MW01629988

EMERGING CULTURE LEADER'S GUIDE

JIMMY LONG

InterVarsity Press
Downers Grove, Illinois

InterVarsity Press
P.O. Box 1400, Downers Grove, IL 60515-1426
World Wide Web: www.ivpress.com
E-mail: mail@ivpress.com

InterVarsity Press® is the book-publishing division of InterVarsity Christian Fellowship/USA®, a student movement active on campus at hundreds of universities, colleges and schools of nursing in the United States of America, and a member movement of the International Fellowship of Evangelical Students. For information about local and regional activities, write Public Relations Dept., InterVarsity Christian Fellowship/USA, 6400 Schroeder Rd., P.O. Box 7895, Madison, WI 53707-7895, or visit the IVCF website at <www.intervarsity.org>.

Cover Design: Cindy Kiple

ISBN 0-8308-2142-2

Printed in the United States of America ∞

P 18 17 16 15 14 13 12 11 10 9 8 7 6 5 4 3 2 1
Y 18 17 16 15 14 13 12 11 10 09 08 07 06 05 04

EMERGING CULTURE LEADER'S GUIDE

Introduction

History is measured by cultural change.

The Bronze Age. The Middle Ages. The Enlightenment. The Modern Age. Each of these eras was so named because of significant changes that distinguish it from the preceding cultures. In the last several decades observers have noticed another significant change. They call it the *postmodern era.* We call it the *emerging culture.*

We may love it, be indifferent to it or even hate it. But the church can't ignore our changing culture since we are part of it. Our youth and young adults are inclined toward the visual, so how can we present sermons they will hear? Worship and music styles are rapidly changing, so how can we find a form that will appeal to everyone in our congregation? People don't respond as readily to our gospel presentations, so how can we effectively show them how appealing the good news of Jesus really is?

The emerging culture won't just blow over. We need to understand it and decide what our role as Christians is within it. The *Emerging Culture Curriculum Kit* will take your group through six experiential modules that explore, analyze and define the emerging culture. But more than that, it will help you shape your ministry for the rest of the twenty-first century. The six modules you will be exploring are

1. Emerging Culture Overview
2. Leadership
3. Witness
4. Communication
5. Context
6. Implications

This introduction is designed to help you, the leader, understand the structure and content of the *Emerging Culture Curriculum Kit* materials. The resources include this leader's guide, the accompanying participant's guides, two CDs and *Emerging Hope* by Jimmy Long. The CDs contain the PowerPoint and video files that you will use in leading groups through this material.

LEADER'S GUIDE

Every module begins with a leader's overview, which includes the following sections:

- Introduction
- Questions Covered
- Content Flow

The "Introduction" and "Questions Covered" sections will give you the big picture of the content in the module. The "Content Flow" section will help you manage your time with the group. Each module will require at least two hours to adequately process the information included in this kit. In "Content Flow," the various parts of each module have been broken down into flexible blocks of time that cover between two and three hours. Please feel free to modify these recommended time sequences as needed.

LEADER'S NOTES

The curriculum for each module contains a variety of learning activities. Usually the first paragraph in a learning activity section is a note for you, the leader. Here you will find suggestions about how to use the immediately following learning segment.

ICONS AND LEARNING ACTIVITIES

In the leader's guide, icons are used to indicate the type of learning activity. The icons are

PRESENTATION

The most common learning activity in each module is a presentation by the leader. In the leader's guide you will find content for each presentation. Sometimes the content is actual text, other times it is in an outline form. In either case the key ideas are described and illustrated. Feel free to add content from your own reading or experience.

BIBLE STUDY

InterVarsity places a high value on learning from the Scripture. The Bible is the basis for all Christian thought and practice. Thus in each module there is a Bible study learning activity. The leader's guide contains notes on some of the Scripture passages and ideas to help summarize main points in the text. We recommend that you study the Scripture passages before leading a group through the passage. The Bible studies all follow a similar format with observation, interpretation and application questions provided. These are variously designed for individual, small group and large group times.

VIDEO CLIP

Within the PowerPoint presentation, video clips of interviews, vignettes and historical overviews enhance the learning process within each module. The leader's preface to the video clip makes suggestions on how to best use the clip. Because the clips are most useful if combined with some kind of group interaction, discussion questions are usually included.

Group Activity

Activities and exercises are included throughout the curriculum to help participants process the information and new ideas within each module.

PowerPoint Presentations

The CDs included in this kit contain a PowerPoint presentation for each module. The PowerPoint presentation includes videos, images, interviews and text corresponding to the leader's and participant's guides. Throughout the leader's guide each PowerPoint slide is designated by a numbered box, which is your notice to advance to the next PowerPoint slide.

When you advance to a PowerPoint slide that has a video presentation, the video will not load automatically. Instead, you will see a black rectangle with the video's title in the lower left-hand corner. This will give you time to introduce the video to the participants. When you are ready to activate the video, simply click in the black rectangle. (Some versions of PowerPoint will require a double-click.)

For technical information about system requirements for the PowerPoint presentation, please read the "Read Me First" document on the first CD-ROM.

LEADER'S ADVANCED PREPARATION

Before you lead a group through the *Emerging Culture Curriculum Kit,* it is recommended that you become thoroughly familiar with all aspects of the curriculum. As the group leader it's important that you read *Emerging Hope* prior to beginning a study of the six modules. This will establish a foundation from which to build a positive group experience. You should also familiarize yourself with the six modules of this leader's guide, working through the PowerPoint slides and videos, reading the Bible studies and answering all of the questions. This will allow you to focus on the group members during your presentation and will facilitate your time management. Likewise, peruse the participant's guide so you can anticipate group member's questions and make any necessary modifications.

All the material in this *Leader's Guide* is not included in the *Participant's Guide.* An asterisk (*) designates material that is included in the *Participant's Guide.* When you see an asterisk, have the participants turn to the appropriate spot to follow along with you.

1
Emerging Culture Overview

OVERVIEW

INTRODUCTION*

This module introduces the emerging culture and describes how it is different from the modern culture. The goal of the curriculum is to help people plan for ministry in the emerging culture. Understanding culture and cultural shifts helps us interact more effectively with people who are part of this emerging culture. This module also includes information about organizational responses to cultural change and suggestions for dealing with change.

QUESTIONS COVERED*

- What is the emerging culture? How do you define it?
- Why is it important to know what the emerging culture is?
- What can or should be my, my church's or my ministry's response to people who are in this emerging culture?

CONTENT FLOW

The following is a suggested arrangement of the learning components in this module. Use the components to customize the training for your audience and time frame.

A. Introduction: Jimmy Long Welcome and Overview (3-5 minutes)

B. Ford Commercials (7-10 minutes)

C. Historical Overview (20-25 minutes)

D. Cultural Paradigm Shifts (15-20 minutes)

E. Will You Be at Home in the Emerging Culture? Quiz (25-35 minutes)

F. Christian Responses to a Changing Culture (30-40 minutes)

G. Church Responses to the Emerging Culture Values (10-15 minutes)

H. Overview Questions (10 minutes)

I. A Preview of Coming Attractions (5-10 minutes)

EMERGING CULTURE: MINISTRY RESOURCES FOR A CHANGING WORLD

A. INTRODUCTION (3-5 MINUTES)

WELCOME AND OVERVIEW by Jimmy Long

Jimmy Long, InterVarsity Christian Fellowship's regional director in the Blue Ridge Region, is the project leader and editor of this curriculum. He and his team worked on this project for more than four years. What you will experience in this curriculum is the fruition of Jimmy's and his team's labor along with the contributions of many other people.

OVERVIEW: MODERN TO EMERGING

MODERN CULTURE TO POSTMODERN CULTURE

LEADER'S NOTE

Click once to advance from "Modern Culture" to "Postmodern Culture."

"The Computer Era." "Leadership by example." "Whatever works for you." "Many paths to God." Wherever we look in our culture today, there are obvious differences from how it was just ten years ago. Leadership styles seem to lean more toward team work and away from hierarchical authority structures.

In many places images take the place of words; we want to see things instead of read about them. Truth? "Truth is what you make it." Experience counts for more than cold facts and scientific explanations. Our culture is changing from a modern to an emerging, postmodern culture. The following car commercials illustrate this shifting culture.

B. FORD COMMERCIALS (7-10 MINUTES)

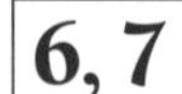

As you view these two commercials, look for similarities and differences. Advertisements try to take advantage of what is important to the culture of the day. What was important in the 1950s? What is important today?

VIDEO QUESTIONS

- How are the two commercials similar? How are they different?

- What might these differences tell us about how culture has changed in the last fifty years?

- How do you normally react to change?

C. HISTORICAL OVERVIEW (20-25 MINUTES)

A Critical Moment in History*

I (Jimmy Long) believe that we are at a critical moment in history. However, some people will disagree with this cultural assessment. There will be even more disagreement on how the church should respond to these cultural shifts. I hope that everyone will be open to what God is doing in our culture. I ask that during this curriculum presentation everyone will continually ask two questions: "What is God doing?" and "How does God want us to be involved?"

9

"Every few hundred years in Western history there occurs a sharp transformation. Within a few short decades, society rearranges itself. . . . Fifty years later, there is a new world. And the people born then cannot even imagine the world in which their grandparents lived and into which their parents were born. We are currently living through just such a transition." Peter Drucker, *Post-Capitalist Society,* p. 126

10

"The 'post' phenomenon is not just a fad. We have truly entered into an epoch fundamentally at variance with anything we have experienced to date. . . . There can be no doubt that the new situation is confronting the Christian church with unprecedented challenges." David Bosch, *Believing in the Future,* p. 1

11

"Many social observers agree that the Western world is in the midst of change. In fact, we are apparently experiencing a cultural shift that rivals the innovations that marked the birth of modernity out of the decay of the Middle Ages: we are in the midst of a transition from the modern to the postmodern era. . . . We see signs that monumental changes are engulfing all aspects of contemporary culture." Stanley Grenz, *A Primer on Postmodernism*, p. 3

History of Change*

Cultural change is not new. History is measured by cultural changes. The Bronze Age. The Middle Ages. The Enlightenment. The Modern Age. These eras are so designated because of significant differences from the cultures that went before. In the last several decades scholars have detected more significant changes occurring in our culture, and they are calling it the *postmodern era.* In this curriculum we will refer to it as the *emerging culture.*

The *modern* culture, with its emphasis on scientific proof, the superiority of the individual and the ultimate power of the word, has been around for about the last five hundred years (since the time of the Reformation). In the last twenty to fifty years there has been a gradual shift away from some of the underlying values of the modern culture. Truth, rather than being scientifically defined, is being defined more often by personal experience. People are becoming less willing to blindly follow a strong leader but seek leaders who work best with teams and are willing to consider opinions other than their own. Attitude shifts like these are the indications of a changing culture.

WHAT DOES THIS MEAN FOR MY CHURCH OR MINISTRY?*

The church has a part in this change as well. We cannot merely sit tight in our own circles and wait for this change to blow over. We need to understand this change and examine what our role is within this changing culture. How should we as Christians respond to these changes? Do our ministries need to change? If they do, in what ways? These are some of the questions we hope to answer in this curriculum.

First, we need to understand that these cultural changes are not chance occurrences. God is continually involved in these changes. How did God use cultural changes in the past to carry out his purposes? The following video will help answer this question.

VIDEO: GOD'S WORK THROUGH HISTORY

LEADER'S NOTE

This video traces cultural changes throughout history. It includes biblical illustrations in which God has caused or used social change to carry out his purposes. The video is intended as an introduction to the *Emerging Culture Curriculum Kit* and raises the question, What might God be doing in our culture today?

VIDEO DISCUSSION*

LEADER'S NOTE

The following questions are included within slide 13.

Click once to advance to each question.

- What did you learn about how God acts during the cultural changes of history?

- What was God's role during these changes?

- In what ways might God be involved in today's cultural changes?

D. CULTURAL PARADIGM SHIFTS (15-20 MINUTES)

LEADER'S NOTE

This section answers the question, What are the major shifts from a modern to our emerging (postmodern) culture? It begins by looking at the four major Western cultural periods since the time of Christ. Then it examines four major transitions from the modern to the emerging culture. Transitions in leadership, communication, witness and context will be the focus for the rest of this curriculum.

HISTORICAL-CULTURAL SHIFTS*

14

In the Western world there have been four major cultural transitions since the death of Christ. The last two transitions have not only had a great affect on the Western world but also have influenced cultures in the Two Thirds World. Due to increasing globalization, the new, emerging culture will have even more of an impact throughout the world.

LEADER'S NOTE

The following four periods are included within slide 14.

Click once to advance to each period.

Hellenistic/Roman A.D. 30 → 600

During this period, which was dominated by Greek thought and Roman power, the Christian church went from a fledgling sect to the dominant religion. The church was characterized by evangelistic zeal.

Medieval A.D. 600 → 1500

In the early Middle Ages the church was in a survivalist mode as the Roman Empire disintegrated and no dominant power took its place. The church became communities that preserved both the faith and civilization. Anselm captured this period with his phrase, "I believe in order that I may understand." In the latter part of this period the church started once again to introduce others to the Christian faith.

Enlightenment/Modern A.D. 1500 → 2000

During the Enlightenment, culture shifted from faith in God to faith in human reasoning. People looked for certainty that they could discover on their own, with little or no dependence on God. Descartes summed up this era with his infamous, "I think, therefore I am."

Postmodern/Emerging A.D. 1968 → ?

The present transition to the emerging postmodern culture involves a shift away from human reason and the autonomous self toward relationship in community. It is a move away from certainty and secular truth to relativism and preferences centered in community. If the emerging culture has a catch phrase it might be, "I belong, therefore I am."

Doug Marlette Cartoon 15

For some people it is very hard to grasp these cultural shifts. This cartoon in a humorous way acknowledges this difficulty.

Modern Culture → Emerging Culture* 

Let's concentrate on the transition between modern and emerging culture. Since we still are in the midst of this transition, it is difficult to specifically define emerging culture. However, we can describe the major changes. The following four shifts describe the essence of the differences between modern and emerging culture.

LEADER'S NOTE

The following cultural shifts are included within slide 16.
Click once to advance to each shift.

Individual → Community

One aspect of the emerging culture the church should be excited about is the movement away from the self (rugged individualism) to the community as the fundamental unit of society. The church was co-opted by modern culture in elevating the individual more than the community. As we see from the very beginning of time, the community (the Trinity, Adam and Eve, the twelve tribes of Israel, the church, etc.) was the basic building block of God. This aspect of emerging culture certainly has not fully arrived, but it is moving in the right direction.

Objective Truth → Subjective Truth

For the last 200 years Western culture believed that universal truth could be discovered without God's involvement. The emerging culture questions that concept; people realize that they cannot find absolute truth through their own efforts. The truth we are left with is highly subjective, depending on the moment or a person's preferences. One positive implication is that this lack of objective truth has caused some people to be more open to exploring spiritual things.

Word → Image

At the beginning of the twentieth century, words dominated our culture. Newspapers, magazines and advertisements used words to communicate their messages. Throughout the past century, word-based media has been relying more and more on images. Most newspapers and magazines have at least one photo or graphic on every page. As we saw earlier, many advertisements rely more heavily on projecting a desired image than on verbally describing the qualities of their product.

Metanarrative → Micronarratives

We largely began the twentieth century with a single story (a metanarrative) of society's progress through history. That story, however, was broken into many stories (micronarratives) derived from the various class, gender, race and ethnic perspectives. While it is true that the unity displayed in the metanarrative never truly existed, the micronarratives that have taken over foster the idea that cultures have never and probably never will be unified.

E. WILL YOU BE AT HOME IN THE EMERGING CULTURE? (25-35 MINUTES)*

17

LEADER'S NOTE

This quiz is a fun exercise that should help the participants discover how modern or postmodern they are. Give participants about fifteen minutes to complete and score the quiz individually, and then bring the group together or in small groups for a short debriefing.

Will you be at home in the emerging culture? Evaluate the following thirty-five statements on a scale of 0 to 5, with 0 meaning you do not agree at all and 5 meaning you very much agree.

1. I believe something when it can be proven scientifically. ____
2. When you get below the surface, people are pretty much the same. ____
3. I'm very interested in how things relate to me. ____
4. I believe in God, but I'm not a big fan of organized religion. ____
5. I'd rather change what I think than lose a friend. ____
6. I tend to use maps and pictures when giving or following directions. ____
7. I think; therefore I am. ____
8. My identity comes from the community where I was raised. ____
9. I choose my words carefully. ____
10. You've got to connect to a group of people you know and trust; no one else understands. ____
11. The world will be a better place by the time I die. ____
12. The issues are much clearer if you aren't emotionally involved. ____
13. The truth can be very complicated. ____

14. I tend to remember sermon illustrations better than the sermon points. ____

15. I think of America as a melting pot of the world's cultures. ____

16. What's most important is my personal relationship with God. ____

17. The role of parents is to raise their children to be independent adults. ____

18. Technology mostly benefits the company that marketed it. ____

19. The book is always better than the movie. ____

20. There are so many different ways of looking at the world. ____

21. I think that sometimes the truth of the matter depends on the situation. ____

22. A chance to make a new discovery should never be passed up. ____

23. I can usually understand what an author means. ____

24. I would choose a job based on the people I'd work with. ____

25. I appreciate a well-organized speech or sermon. ____

26. I am comfortable in front of a screen. ____

27. I find the scenes in movies before 1990 to be too long. ____

28. It's not that important to know your neighbors. ____

29. My denomination's theology is closest to Scripture. ____

30. I follow written instructions with ease. ____

31. I have a high appreciation for logical consistency. ____

32. People are no better or worse now than they have ever been. ____

33. I usually enjoy movies based on books. ____

34. It's important to find people with whom I can share my most intimate thoughts and feelings. ____

35. I find it's easy for people to misunderstand one another. ____

Now score yourself on the next page by putting the value you gave each question in the score sheet box with the same number. Total the column of numbers and plot your score on the corresponding graph. The x-axis represents postmodern values. The y-axis represents modern values.

18-21

Objectivity-Subjectivity

Y-Axis: Objectivity

1	☐	3	☐
12	☐	5	☐
23	☐	13	☐
29	☐	21	☐
31	☐	35	☐
Total	☐	Total	☐

X-Axis: Subjectivity

25 20 15 10 5 0
MODERN
POSTMODERN
Objectivity
0 5 10 15 20 25
Subjectivity

Debrief Notes

This quiz measures your tendency toward more modern or postmodern characteristics. The closer the dot is to the center line the more balanced a person is between modern and postmodern. The further away from the center line, the stronger a person's tendency is in a particular category.

Individual-Community

Y-Axis: Autonomous Individual

7	☐	5	☐
12	☐	8	☐
16	☐	10	☐
17	☐	24	☐
28	☐	34	☐
Total	☐	Total	☐

X-Axis: Community

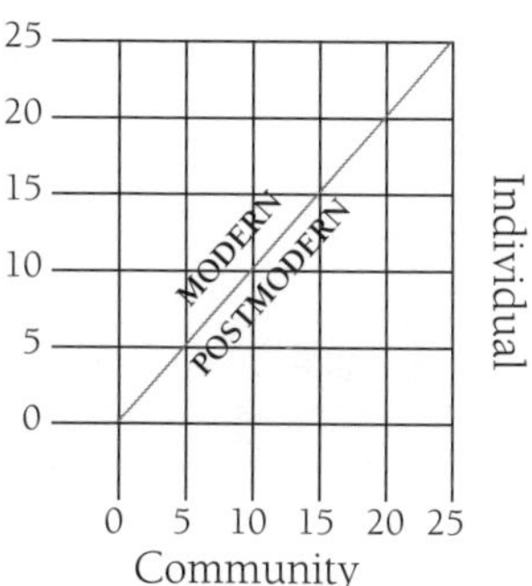

Word-Image

Y-Axis: Word

9	☐	6	☐
19	☐	14	☐
23	☐	26	☐
25	☐	27	☐
30	☐	33	☐
Total	☐	Total	☐

X-Axis: Image

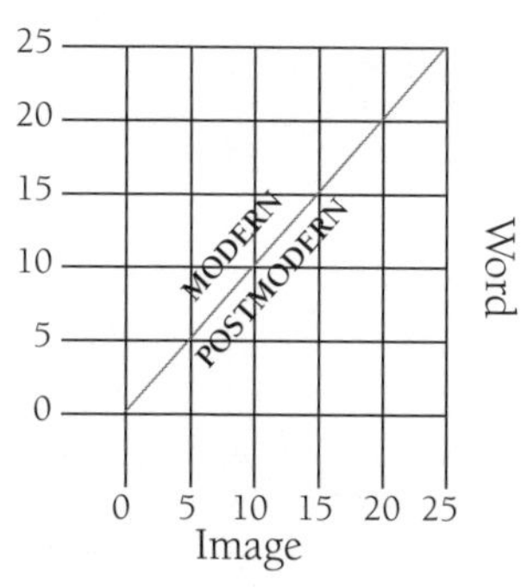

Metanarrative-Micronarratives

Y-Axis: Metanarrative

2	☐	4	☐
11	☐	18	☐
15	☐	20	☐
22	☐	32	☐
29	☐	35	☐
Total	☐	Total	☐

X-Axis: Micronarratives

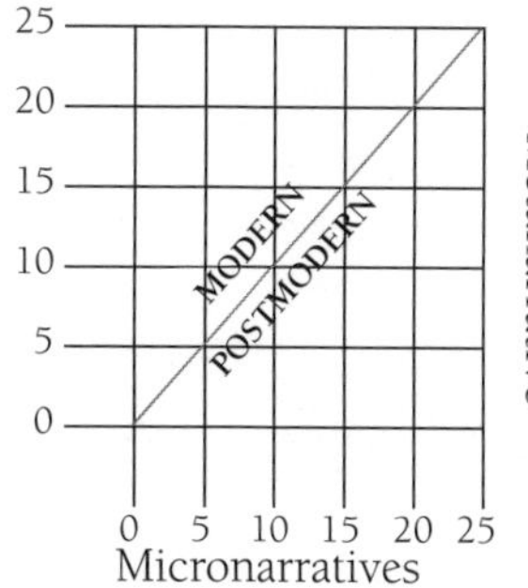

EXERCISE QUESTIONS* 

- What did you learn about yourself?

- From this exercise, do you think you will be more or less at home in this emerging culture?

F. CHRISTIAN RESPONSES TO A CHANGING CULTURE (30-40 MINUTES)*

LEADER'S NOTE

This session discusses the most common responses that churches or ministries have had to cultural change. The last ten minutes are for journaling or small group discussion. Participants can analyze which response most closely describes their own response or the response of their church or ministry.

RESPONSE TO A CHANGING CULTURE 23

- How have Christians responded to change in the past?

- What are the various ways churches and ministries are responding to cultural change today?

*Unchanging Tradition** 24
Some people see tradition as paramount; they usually believe there is no need to change. They often see their own tradition as going back to the time of Christ, not just as a historical and cultural development. An example of this kind of thinking is those who say, "If the King James Bible was good enough for Jesus, it is good enough for me."

*Developmental Phase** 25
Others see the new ideas of younger people as temporary or a phase they will grow out of. Eventually the young will be like their elders. Certainly there is validity to this perspective. However, in times of cultural change, we often realize too late that younger folks are not going to grow out of it.

*Generational Transition** 26

These people see cultural changes, especially those of the last ten to fifteen years, as a result of the changing generations—Boomers, Gen-X, Millennials. Those who hold this position see the changes as transient effects without lasting impact beyond one generation. They view culture as remaining essentially the same, with occasional variations on the surface level. People who see cultural changes primarily though this lens fail to realize that the concept of generational transition is almost exclusively a Western phenomenon. Most people in other cultures have no concept of generational transition.

*Emerging Culture: Fortress Mentality**  27

People coming from this view see cultural change coming, and they believe that change is something to avoid and protect others from. They may be willing to change, but not to the extent of the emerging culture. Certainly, we need to be wise and withstand negative cultural influences. However, God sometimes brings about cultural change to renew the church and prepare people to receive the gospel.

*Emerging Culture: Prophetic Voice**  28

Some people definitely see the cultural shift taking place, and they do not want to hide from it. While they see some of these changes as positive, they believe the church's primary role is to protect those within its circles, warning them of the negative consequences of this changing culture.

*Emerging Culture: Mission Opportunity**  29

Instead of dwelling on the negative consequences of cultural change, some people perceive that God is providentially overseeing some of these changes to accomplish his purposes. So instead of seeing their primary role as warning the church, they are looking for mission opportunities for the gospel to go forward in this changing culture.

DIETER ZANDER INTERVIEW 30

LEADER'S NOTE

Dieter Zander was one of the first Gen-X pastors of Southern California in the early 1990s. From there Dieter became the pastor of Axis, Willow Creek's ministry to Gen-Xers and other postmodern people. Presently Dieter is involved in a ministry helping churches in the San Francisco area know how to minister in the emerging culture.

People respond in a variety of ways to the emerging culture. Some see no change and wonder why we are spending time talking about such matters. Others see the change as temporary and not a major paradigm shift. We are going to hear from one person who went through his own transition in how he viewed these cultural changes.

VIDEO QUESTIONS 31

- What do we learn about Dieter's journey?
- What were some of the key turning points in Dieter's journey?
- What have been the key points in your journey in this time of cultural transition?

SELF-ASSESSMENT* 32

Six Responses to the Emerging Culture

LEADER'S NOTE

The following responses are included within slide 32.

Click once to advance to each response.

- Unchanging Tradition
- Developmental Phase
- Generational Transition
- Emerging Culture: Fortress
- Emerging Culture: Prophetic
- Emerging Culture: Mission Opportunity

GROUP DISCUSSION 33

LEADER'S NOTE

Using the above six responses, have participants answer the following questions in writing and then share the results within their small group.

1. In order of priority from one to three, rank the three *primary* ways people in your church or ministry respond to the changing culture. (For example: 1. generational transition, 2. emerging culture: fortress, 3. developmental phase)

2. Rank yourself and compare it with how you rated your church or ministry.

3. Where would you like to see yourself and your church or ministry?

G. CHURCH RESPONSES TO THE EMERGING CULTURE VALUES (10-15 MINUTES)* 34

What should be the Christian response to each of these cultural values?

CHURCH RESPONSES TO THE EMERGING CULTURE VALUES 35

LEADER'S NOTE

The following responses are included within slide 35.

Click once to advance to each response.

MODERN CULTURE	EMERGING CULTURE	CHRISTIAN RESPONSE
Individual	*Community*	*Christian Community*

As Christians we should rejoice that the culture is moving away from individualism and moving toward community. God created us to live in community. However, what we see in the culture today is not true Christian community but tribal-like groupings that tend to be separate from other groups. Christians need to enter into true Christian community, caring for each other and reaching out to others outside the community.

Word	*Image*	*Word & Image*

In a culture that is fascinated by television and movies, the power of image is easy to see. And yet to non-Christians the gospel appears stuck in the realm of tolerable but hardly attractive words. The emerging culture wants to see and experience, not read someone else's description. We need to use both words and images to communicate the power and relevance of the gospel.

Objective Truth	*Subjective Truth*	*Embodied Apologetics*

In a culture that says there is no objective truth, only preferences based on experience and opinion, the church needs to allow people to experience the gospel through the lives of Christians. The best apologetic will be to show people the changing power of the gospel in caring Christian communities that are willing to include those who are not Christians. As the non-Christians experience the truth lived out in our lives, they become more open to hearing and accepting the truth themselves.

Metanarrative	*Micronarratives*	*God's Kingdom Story*

In a society that is fragmented into racial, generational and religious groups, there is no single unifying story of human history. Instead, each group has its own unique and correct version of history. Into this chaos the gospel is frequently unwelcome because it does not match a particular person's history. We must seek to display the unifying nature of the gospel, that it is in fact intended for every person and group and not a separate history of itself.

H. OVERVIEW QUESTIONS (10 MINUTES)*

36

- In the past, how has God interacted with cultural changes?

- How is God interacting today with this transition into the emerging culture?

- How do you emotionally respond to this emerging culture?

- What do you (we) still need to learn about this emerging culture?

I. A PREVIEW OF COMING ATTRACTIONS (5-10 MINUTES)

37

In the remainder of the curriculum we will look at the following five modules.

LEADER'S NOTE

The following modules are included within slide 37.

Click once to advance to each module.

MODULE	MODERN TENDENCY		POSTMODERN TENDENCY
Leadership	*Self*	→	*Community*

Leadership styles and methods are changing. Mostly gone now are the days of a strict hierarchical structure where orders are passed down the chain of command from a rarely seen but "always right" boss. Instead, leaders are becoming more conscious of others involved in the decision-making process and the long-term results of those decisions. The second module looks specifically at four aspects of leadership and how they can be used most effectively within the emerging culture.

Witness	*Objective Truth*	→	*Subjective Truth*

Witnessing has always been a primary concern of the church, but its evangelistic methods have varied throughout history. Within the emerging culture, some of the methods of the last fifty years have become less effective. This module looks at the questions people are asking about Christianity and some of the effective ways to deal with these questions.

Communication *Word* → *Image*

Communicating the same message to many people has always been a challenge. The written, printed or projected word has been the solution to this problem for the last several centuries. Today's emerging culture prefers the drawn, painted or projected image—television, movies, animation—to the static word. Module three addresses the advantages and disadvantages of using both words and images, and suggests ways to combine the two to create the most effective communication.

Context *Metanarrative* → *Micronarratives*

Rather than look at history as a unified whole that can be told from a single perspective, it is becoming more common to look at different parts of history from various perspectives. This module addresses the use of those different perspectives to create a more unified view of the world that can be a more effective way to identify with those in the emerging culture.

Implications *Programs* → *Relationships*

To bring all these pieces together, this last module looks at what this information can mean to your church or ministry. Indeed, change is occurring in the culture. How will you and your church or ministry respond to these changes?

Select Resources

Books

Emerging Hope (chaps. 1-3) by Jimmy Long
Challenge of Postmodernism edited by David Dockery
ChurchNext by Eddie Gibbs
Death of the Church by Mike Regele
Gospel in a Pluralist Society by Lesslie Newbigin
Primer on Postmodernism by Stanley Grenz
Transforming Mission by David Bosch

Articles

"The Evolution of Gen X Ministry," *Re:Generation Quarterly,* fall 1999, by Dieter and Valerie Zander
"Leading into the Unknown," *Leadership,* fall 1999, by Eric Reed
"Ministering with My Generation," *Leadership,* fall 2000, by Eric Reed
"Navigating Cultural Currents," *Leadership,* fall 2000, by Soong-Chan Rah
"What the World Needs Now," *Leadership,* spring 1993, by Leonard Sweet

2 Leadership

OVERVIEW

Introduction*

This module addresses the emerging culture shift from viewing and practicing leadership as a quality found in a single individual to the agreement and decisions of a community or group. While modernity values a strong, hierarchical leadership, postmoderns value a team-based and community supportive leadership that delegates responsibility broadly.

Questions Covered*

- What are the differences between modern and emerging leadership?
- What does Scripture say about leadership?
- What are some of the specific aspects of leadership that can be most effective in this emerging culture?
- What methods and styles are beneficial in our own leadership context?

Content Flow

The following is a suggested arrangement of the learning components in this module. Use the components to customize the training for your audience and time frame.

A. Introduction (5 minutes)

B. Leighton Ford Interview (10-15 minutes)

C. Young People on Leadership (10-15 minutes)

D. Leadership Changes in the Emerging Culture (15-20 minutes)

E. Biblical Principles for Leadership in the Emerging Culture (30-40 minutes)

Optional: Case Study: Leadership in Emerging Culture (20-30 minutes)

F. Four Dynamics of Emerging Leadership: A Closer Look (40-60 minutes)

G. All About the Journey (10-15 minutes)

H. Leadership Questions (10 minutes)

LEADERSHIP: FROM INDIVIDUAL TO COMMUNITY 

A. INTRODUCTION (5 MINUTES)

LEADER'S NOTE

This introduction is a brief overview of the topics covered in the leadership module. If you have a personal example to tie in with this general information, it may be helpful to include it as you introduce this topic to the participants.

LEADERSHIP DYNAMICS*

There may have been a time when leaders commanded their subordinates based solely on their title or position. However, as our culture morphs, the expectations of followers and leaders are far more complex. In this module, we will look at four changing aspects of leadership:

- Community
- Character
- Vision
- Journey

In the emerging culture, *community* and relationships are critically important; emerging leaders are very concerned about all the people within their organization. *Character* has always been a relatively important part of true leadership, but in the emerging culture character is central to the authentication of the leader. Emerging leaders focus on the *vision* (or image) that tells them where the group is going. Many young, emerging leaders see themselves on a developmental journey, and often the *journey* itself is as important to them as the goal.

OUR PROCESS

In this module we will listen to a variety of young leaders and examine situations that any of us might encounter. Then, looking at Scripture we will find instructions and examples about leadership dynamics. We will also have the opportunity to learn from each other—because in the emerging culture, community is an important way we learn. But before we go any further, let's listen to what one Christian leader says about this transition from modern to emerging leadership.

B. LEIGHTON FORD INTERVIEW (10-15 MINUTES) 2

As someone who has been a Christian leader for many years and whose mission for the last twenty years has been to raise up future Christian leaders, Leighton Ford is in a unique position to give us a glimpse of the emerging leadership.

LEIGHTON FORD DISCUSSION

LEADER'S NOTE

The three questions are included within slide 3.

Click once to advance to each question.

- What are some of the changes in leadership that Leighton identifies?
- What are some of the characteristics of emerging leaders?
- Where might modern and emerging leaders experience tension?

C. YOUNG PEOPLE ON LEADERSHIP (10-15 MINUTES)

LEADER'S NOTE

This video comprises comments on leadership by young people. These people reflect both modern and postmodern perspectives. After the video, ask questions to help people think about their own style and the emerging leadership style.

As we look at leadership in the emerging culture, it's important that we listen to what young people have to say because they are the vanguard of the transition into emerging culture. Listen to their perspective. How is it similar or different to your understanding of leadership?

LEADERSHIP VIDEO

PERSPECTIVE ON LEADERSHIP 5

- What did or didn't these young people say that you expected to hear?
- What characteristics were desired or respected in a leader?
- What do you look for in a leader?

D. LEADERSHIP CHANGES IN THE EMERGING CULTURE (15-20 MINUTES)*

LEADER'S NOTE

This section looks first at the developing changes in leadership between the modern and emerging cultures. The leadership changes are evident at several levels. We can see these changes most clearly between people who closely identify with either the modern or postmodern culture. However, there are many people who identify with some aspects of both. Next we will explore more closely four dynamics of leadership in the emerging culture—community, character, vision and journey.

Changes in Leadership

If we are going to increasingly minister within an emerging-culture context, we need to understand the changes in leadership style that are taking place between the modern and emerging cultures. Even if we are more modern ourselves, we need to become aware of these differences so we can effectively minister as we interact with postmodern people. In addition, those of us who are immersed in the emerging culture need to understand where the more established and modern leaders are coming from in our church or ministries.

Transitioning Leadership*

LEADER'S NOTE

The following "changes" are included within slide 6.

Click once to progress through "Modern Culture" and "Emerging Culture" changes.

Modern Culture	**Emerging Culture**
Individual leader	Team leadership
Task-oriented	Community-oriented
Positional authority	Earned authority
Perfect leader	Broken leader
Building structures	Developing vision
Control	Empower
Destination	Journey
Aspire to leadership	Inspire to leadership

This list is neither exhaustive nor authoritative. However, it highlights the trends in the emerging leadership. Moving from the individual leader to team leadership and community does coincide with the biblical descriptions of the church as a community. As we face an ongoing task, we leaders will need to recognize that developing the members of the taskforce into a community is critical. In the emerging culture we must recognize that holding a leadership position does not mean people will automatically follow or trust the leader. Trust has to be earned through relationships. Trust will be earned in part as leaders acknowledge their imperfection and brokenness. Henri Nouwen describes the emerging leader as a "wounded healer." People in the emerging culture not only need a vision to live for but empowerment to help develop that vision, part of which is a sense that the whole team is on this journey together. Finally, in the emerging culture fewer people aspire to leadership because (1) they do not feel like they have necessary leadership characteristics, or (2) they believe as leaders they will be automatically excluded from the community. Thus we will have to be more sensitive and proactive in encouraging people to become leaders.

DYNAMICS OF EMERGING LEADERSHIP* 7

The following are four dynamics of leadership that will be highlighted as we look at how to develop sustainable leadership in the emerging culture:

LEADER'S NOTE

The following four dynamics are included within slide 7.

Click once to advance to each.

Community

The optimum environment for leadership is no longer individuals with specific responsibilities. Emerging leaders operate best as part of a community. Community, however, is more than a team; it involves true friendship and authentic cost. Communities have an organic and dynamic edge that makes them synergistic—the community as a whole is greater than the sum of its individual members. For people that are part of the emerging culture, the call to leadership is a call to community.

Character

Often we pursue natural leaders and help them develop gifts and skills for ministry, but we leave them impoverished in terms of character development. We encourage them to use their skills before their character has been honed. Thus they have positional authority without earning true authority by means of their own good character. Such leaders project an image of "perfection," never admitting their own needs. At times we overlook people with strong character in order to pursue leaders with more obvious gifts. This lack of character can produce one or more negative scenarios:

- The leader may make decisions based strictly on his or her own skills and performance, sacrificing other people in order to look better.

- A leader focused on skills and performance may not be able to handle failure; thus he or she will train others to produce at all costs.
- The followers or fellow team members may reject the leader's authority because his or her position of authority has not been earned through character development.
- The leader who does not cultivate his or her spiritual life but nevertheless continues to excel may end up feeling used by the organization he or she is serving.

Vision

Emerging leaders are motivated by a passion for something more than the small and ordinary life. To win a beachhead in leadership development, we need to flame the emerging leader's passion for great things, for the extension of the kingdom of God. Specific tasks are not exciting to emerging leaders unless they feel those tasks are fundamentally connected to the larger vision. As long as the vision is clear and prominent, emerging leaders will flourish.

Sluggish leaders will not respond to a heart-to-heart discussion of discipline, duty or commitment; they need us to describe and illustrate our ministry's vision. Through storytelling and imagination the vision must be recast and redescribed time and again. This will have a reinvigorating effect on young leaders, and they will reprioritize their life and ministry around the vision.

Journey

Young leaders are increasingly living extreme and intense lives of passionate commitment. They know they are on a journey, but to where? Where will their own passions take them? Who will serve as a guide for their journey? Will their ministry partners encourage them as they sometimes take two steps forward and three steps back? Often the way we understand our own traits and those of others will define beginning points and destinations for our journey.

All Christians are on a journey, but who or what will direct emerging leaders? Can we help them define their beginning points and guide them toward a fulfilling destination? If we can walk with emerging leaders on their "forward and back again" journey, we hopefully will see a healthy, sustainable leadership culture grow in the next generation.

Discussion on Leadership Changes in the Emerging Culture*

- What are some of the key changes in leadership between modern and emerging cultures?
- Are there other changes that need to be explored?
- Why are the four dynamics of community, character, vision and journey so crucial in the emerging culture?

E. BIBLICAL PRINCIPLES FOR LEADERSHIP IN THE EMERGING CULTURE (30-40 MINUTES)*

9

LEADER'S NOTE

The two passages, John 13:1-16 and John 15:8-17, in this Scripture study work together to give further insight into aspects of community, character, vision and journey. Give the participants ten minutes to read through the passage. Then go through the observation, interpretation and application questions.

Peter and Jesus are the main characters in these passages. Their interaction provides the content of the study. As you study these passages think about the following questions:

- What is the importance of community and character? How do these dynamics interact?
- How is vision communicated and what is its importance?
- What are the evidences of journey? How does this help you understand the dynamic of journey?

John 13:1-16

Now before the festival of the Passover, Jesus knew that his hour had come to depart from this world and go to the Father. Having loved his own who were in the world, he loved them to the end. [2]The devil had already put it into the heart of Judas son of Simon Iscariot to betray him. And during supper [3]Jesus, knowing that the Father had given all things into his hands, and that he had come from God and was going to God, [4]got up from the table, took off his outer robe, and tied a towel around himself. [5]Then he poured water into a basin and began to wash the disciples' feet and to wipe them with the towel that was tied around him. [6]He came to Simon Peter, who said to him, "Lord, are you going to wash my feet?" [7]Jesus answered, "You do not know now what I am doing, but later you will understand." [8]Peter said to him, "You will never wash my feet." Jesus answered, "Unless I wash you, you have no share with me." [9]Simon Peter said to him, "Lord, not my feet only but also my hands and my head!" [10]Jesus said to him, "One who has bathed does not need to wash, except for the feet, but is entirely clean. And you are clean, though not all of you." [11]For he knew who was to betray him; for this reason he said, "Not all of you are clean."

[12]After he had washed their feet, had put on his robe, and had returned to the table, he said to them, "Do you know what I have done to you? [13]You call me Teacher and Lord—

Commentary

In this passage we see Peter in the foreground. Peter tries to single himself out. But Jesus calls him to the community. Peter's character is being shaped by Jesus' rebuke and challenge. Jesus is laying out a tangible expression of his mission: communal servant leadership. He wants the disciples to emulate his leadership by serving one another. If the love Jesus has for them doesn't transform their community, how will it transform the world? Jesus is able to take a long-term view of Peter's character development. He knows that remaining in community with the other disciples is part of this.

and you are right, for that is what I am. [14]So if I, your Lord
and Teacher, have washed your feet, you also ought to wash
one another's feet. [15]For I have set you an example, that you
also should do as I have done to you. [16]Very truly, I tell you,
servants are not greater than their master, nor are messen-
gers greater than the one who sent them."

John 15:8-17

[8]My Father is glorified by this, that you bear much fruit and
become my disciples. [9]As the Father has loved me, so I have
loved you; abide in my love. [10]If you keep my commandments, you will abide in my love, just as I have kept my Father's commandments and abide in his love. [11]I have said
these things to you so that my joy may be in you, and that
your joy may be complete.

[12]This is my commandment, that you love one another as I
have loved you. [13]No one has greater love than this, to lay
down one's life for one's friends. [14]You are my friends if you do
what I command you. [15]I do not call you servants any longer,
because the servant does not know what the master is doing;
but I have called you friends, because I have made known to
you everything that I have heard from my Father. [16]You did
not choose me but I chose you. And I appointed you to go and
bear fruit, fruit that will last, so that the Father will give you
whatever you ask him in my name. [17]I am giving you these
commands so that you may love one another.

Commentary

Jesus is clear about what his vision for the disciples is. In love he wants them to lay down their lives in the same way he is about to lay his own life down for them. The details of their call is becoming more clear: Jesus calls them friends rather than servants because he wants them to join with him and the Father in missional community.

Observation Questions*

10

1. How is Peter in the foreground in the first passage?

2. What is the main focus of the second passage?

3. Is there a sense of time passing, or is this a one-time, static statement?

Interpretation Questions*

1. Each time Peter attempts to single himself out with Jesus, he is called back to community. How is Peter's character being shaped by Jesus' rebuke and challenge?

2. In John 15, what is Jesus saying about the character of a missional community? How are his actions reinforcing his teaching? How are the developing leaders invited to or included in the missional community?

3. What are the origins of Jesus' missional community?

4. How do community, character, vision and journey appear in the passages?

APPLICATION QUESTIONS*

12

1. How is leadership a call to Jesus and to servanthood within our community?

2. How is Jesus instituting ways of relating to the collective leadership community?

3. Knowing that Peter would deny him, Jesus still loved him and involved him. In what ways can we have a "journey" perspective on the leaders we are currently serving? How will we trust them with the vision and invite them to partnership even when we anticipate their shortcomings?

4. How are we invited into this missional community?

(Optional)

CASE STUDY: LEADERSHIP IN EMERGING CULTURE
(20-30 MINUTES)*

LEADER'S NOTE

The following case study is designed to bring together questions and ideas discussed so far. In this key part of the training, participants build confidence and understanding by applying what they have learned. This segment is time elastic and depends on the length of discussion in the small and large groups.

This section helps participants analyze a situation between a church leader and a small group leader who connects strongly with the emerging culture. The issues most obvious in this scenario are related to community and vision. Be sure to draw out the aspects of character and journey as well.

Break the people into groups of three to five for discussion. Use "Further Data" and "Broader Issues" to help the groups think about effective solutions. After each group has had a chance to discuss the scenario, have a large group discussion about what people came up with or learned.

Situation

Rachel is the leader of the small group ministry at a church with many younger people. She is planning a leadership training day for small group leaders (SGLT). She contacts people to remind them about the event and to find out who is coming. Dave is a young leader who has been committed to both his small group and evangelism with the Frisbee golf team. Dave e-mails her and describes his dilemma.

Rachel,
I'm having trouble deciding about this Saturday's SGLT. I know I need to be with the other leaders and that the training would help me be a stronger biblical leader for my small group, but I said I'd help the non-Christian guys I'm reaching out to with a workday at the Frisbee golf course. I feel conflicted about which group of people I should be with on Saturday. I'm leaning toward spending Saturday with the Frisbee golf team. What do you think?
Dave

WHAT WOULD YOU SAY TO EACH OF THEM?

FURTHER DATA

- ***Dave's Leadership Experience***
  Dave stepped in as a small group leader because the former leader of the group moved out of the area. Dave is a natural leader with lots of energy and insight, but he hasn't received small group leader training. The church runs SGLT only twice a year.

- ***Dave's Communities***
  Dave sees his call to leadership as a call to the community of his small group, not necessarily to the larger church. He also feels he has a call to witness to the community he has with the Frisbee golf team. The SGLT adds a third community, the small group leaders community, and it asks him to choose between his small group and his Frisbee golf team. The small group would probably benefit from his training, the Frisbee people would benefit from his involvement, and he would benefit from being in the small group leaders community.

- ***Rachel's Vision***
  Rachel is deeply committed to evangelism. Six months ago she led a training day for evangelism. Dave came, and as a result he has begun to actively reach out to his friends at the Frisbee golf course. She is also committed to strong training for young leaders. She believes the training would help Dave with his small group and help him witness to his non-Christian friends.

- ***Rachel and Dave's Relationship***
  The relationship between Rachel and Dave is one of leader/mentor to follower/student. Rachel leads the small group ministry and, aside from his small group members, is Dave's main connection to the church. Dave is a

new small group leader and as such is willing to learn. Dave and Rachel respect and appreciate each other for the roles they have. Dave sees Rachel as personal and energetic, and can sense her commitment to see him grow as a spiritual leader. Rachel can see that Dave connects with the small group ministry's vision and has tremendous potential.

WHAT ADVICE WOULD YOU GIVE EACH NOW?

WHAT DEEPER ISSUES ARE PROBABLY INVOLVED?

HOW MIGHT THE SITUATION BE RESOLVED?

BROADER ISSUES

Dealing with Multiple Communities

If Dave feels that a commitment to be a small group leader will require him to give up his outreach to the Frisbee people, he probably won't be a long-term leader. By being flexible and affirming both commitments, Rachel can confirm her commitment to help him grow in godly character while reiterating the vision of the small group ministry. If she is flexible with Dave because of his outside commitment to evangelism, he will likely be flexible in his commitments to both communities.

Involving the Community in the Decision

Dave could ask his small group to pray about his decision. He could also let the Frisbee guys know about this other commitment on Saturday—consulting them could raise spiritual questions on their part!

ANALYSIS

Rachel's Motivation

Dave's need for leadership training could be a task-oriented and individualistic approach. On the other hand, Dave's interests are for his communities and for his own character development. The training might be beneficial to both his character and his small group members. The training could also help him witness to his non-Christian friends. These questions connect with Dave's interests—balancing different communities, the importance of vision and developing character.

Dave's Questions

If Dave merely shows up to play Frisbee but isn't willing to help with the workday, what will his friends think? Will training be beneficial enough to pass up this chance to be involved with the Frisbee team?

It's All About Character

Rachel wants to help Dave follow God's leading regarding Saturday. He sees his need to be both a stronger Bible study leader and faithful in evangelism. Dave would describe these needs in terms of commitment ("I said I would") rather than obligation ("I'm required to"). He loves the people in his small group and wants to be a better leader for them. He also loves his non-Christian friends and wants to serve them by helping at the workday. These are the marks of a wonderful small group leader!

What About Community?

Dave is missing the connection to the larger leadership community. If he continues to lead without being connected to other small group leaders, what will happen to him? If Rachel is his only connection to the larger church community, what happens if she leaves? Without a strong connection to the larger leadership community, Dave's vision and leadership may not grow in the right directions.

POSSIBLE SOLUTIONS

1. Half and Half

Move the training earlier in the morning so Dave can attend the first part. Then have the other leaders pray for him as he helps the Frisbee people. This way he can be involved in both communities.

2. One, Then the Other

Have Dave go to the Frisbee workday, and then have one of the leaders who was at the training go over the material with Dave. This way Dave connects with someone on the leadership team without sacrificing his time with the Frisbee people.

3. Three-point

Have Dave attend the training event, but go out at lunch to bring food to the Frisbee people. Some of the other small group leaders or members of Dave's small group could also go. This would bring all three of Dave's communities together.

F. FOUR DYNAMICS OF EMERGING LEADERSHIP: A CLOSER LOOK (40-60 MINUTES)

1. COMMUNITY (10-15 MINUTES)

LEADER'S NOTE

In the following video, leaders comment on how they see community in their own leadership experiences. After showing the video you may want to give people a few minutes to make observations and comment on their own experiences.

COMMUNITY VIDEO 13

COMMUNITY DISCUSSION QUESTIONS* 14

- How do you identify with the comments of these leaders?
- Why is developing community so important for leaders in the emerging culture?
- What did you learn from the video or from your own experience on how to build a community of leaders?
- If the basic unit of leadership development were community rather than the individual, how would your training events and processes change?

2. CHARACTER (10-15 MINUTES)

LEADER'S NOTE

In the following video, leaders discuss the issues of character and skill. After showing the video, give people a few minutes to make observations and comment on their own experiences.

CHARACTER VIDEO 

CHARACTER DISCUSSION QUESTIONS* 16

- What character issues are mentioned in this video?
- In a culture that distrusts authority, why is character so important?
- Why is character more important than skill? How do you see character and skill working together in leadership?
- How do you develop the character of future leaders?

3. VISION (10-15 MINUTES)

LEADER'S NOTE

In the following video, leaders talk about the need to have vision and to communicate that vision to those they lead. After viewing the video, have participants discuss how this video relates to what they have seen and experienced as they have led others.

VISION VIDEO 

VISION DISCUSSION QUESTIONS* 18

- How do leaders in the video talk about vision?

- Why is it especially important for leaders to develop vision as we move into this emerging culture?

- How does the leader develop vision in this emerging culture?

- What are some of the characteristics of vision that are critical in an emerging culture?

4. JOURNEY (10-15 MINUTES)

LEADER'S NOTE

In the following video, leaders analyze how leadership is a continuing journey. After watching the video, discuss some of the steps you have taken and anticipate you will take on this journey.

JOURNEY VIDEO 

JOURNEY DISCUSSION QUESTIONS* 20

- In this emerging culture, why is "journey" an appropriate description of a leadership team?

- What does this journey look like?

- For emerging leaders, why is the journey just as important as the destination?

G. ALL ABOUT THE JOURNEY (10-15 MINUTES) 21

EMERGING LEADERSHIP DEVELOPMENT

LEADER'S NOTE

The following points are included within slide 21.

Click once to advance to each.

Beginning Points

When we approach the emerging leadership as a problem to solve, we only see the negative traits: leaders who in our estimation exhibit signs of having a "bad case of postmodernism."

Scattered
Passion

They seem enormously scattered and passionate at the same time. The leaders we work with sometimes seem hesitant about or rebellious toward institutional authority. We find that we spend significant energy building trust in order for ministry to even be possible.

Fear
Brokenness

Addressing leaders' fear and brokenness is important, but we must broaden our ministries if we want to be balanced and focused for the long-term. We need to identify the positive traits and instincts in emerging leaders. Leaders today are open, flexible and change oriented. They are intense and passionate about life. When we begin to corral the scattered and harness the passionate, we enjoy and celebrate the flexibility and intensity of the emerging leaders around us. We access a vitality that enables hope and faithfulness in ministry. We also become learners as well as leaders, and that translates into authenticity and trust with the young people we lead.

A Process of Journey 22

When we begin to embrace the adventure and motion of the emerging leadership journey, we are apt to discover how the beginning traits develop into other traits along their journey. Focusing on these traits shows how young leaders can develop on the journey.

LEADER'S NOTE

The following points are included within slide 22.

Click once to advance from each of the "Beginning Points" to the steps "On the Journey."

Beginning Points	**On the Journey**
from scattered	to focused
from passion	to worship
from fear	to trust
from brokenness	to healing

But the journey of emerging leaders has even more potential. We can dream even bigger. We must envision the journey of the emerging leaders and dream about what they will become when they are spiritually formed. Over a period of time they will move from being scattered to focused and eventually to faithfulness. Their passion for life will turn to worship of God and eventually to mission of God. Their fear will lead to trust and then real partnership. As we help broken people enter communities where they can be healed, these communities will become communities of embodied hope, a welcome place for all people.

LEADER'S NOTE

Have the participants fill in the blanks to "The Process of Journey" in their participant's guide.

---

*The Process of Journey** 23

Beginning Points	On the Journey	End of Journey
from scattered	to focused	to faithfulness
from passion	to worship	to mission
from fear	to trust	to partnership
from brokenness	to healing	to embodied hope

H. LEADERSHIP QUESTIONS (10 MINUTES)* 24

- How have your assumptions about leadership in the emerging culture been challenged?

- What is the relationship between community and leadership?

- How might your leadership structures and leadership development need to change in light of the emerging culture?

Select Resources

Books

Emerging Hope (chap. 8) by Jimmy Long
Good to Great by Jim Collins

Articles

"Emerging Values," *Leadership,* summer 2003, by Brian McLaren
"From My Vision to Our Vision," *Leadership,* summer 2000, by Paul Ford

3
Witness

OVERVIEW

Introduction*

This module addresses a shift in the emerging culture from a concern for absolute truth to a desire for belonging. This shift affects evangelism. This witness module explores questions and values significant to the emerging culture, and gives practical ideas about discussing spiritual issues with people today.

Questions Covered*

- Where does evangelism fit in my heart and life?
- Who am I likely to be reaching?
- What questions and attitudes do people have today?
- How can I answer some of these questions?
- What kind of answers would be most effective?

Content Flow

The following is a suggested arrangement of the learning components in this module. Use the components to customize the training for your audience and time frame.

A. Introduction (5-10 minutes)
B. Implications for Witness (10-15 minutes)
C. Becky Pippert Interview (10-15 minutes)
D. Scripture Study (30-40 minutes)
E. Daniel Hill Interview (15 minutes)
F. Questions of and Responses to Modern and Emerging People (15-20 minutes)
G. The Spiritual Journey of Emerging People (10-15 minutes)
H. Lessons from the Past: Roman Versus Celtic Model (10-15 minutes)
I. Conversion in the Emerging Culture (15-20 minutes)
J. Witness Questions (5-10 minutes)

WITNESS: BELONGING BEFORE BELIEVING 1

A. INTRODUCTION (5-10 MINUTES) 

LEADER'S NOTE

The following ideas and the *Titanic* movie metaphor help draw participants into the content of this module on evangelism. You may also want to use personal stories that shed light on the following ideas.

Each of the following points are included within slide 2.

Click once for each point.

A CULTURAL EARTHQUAKE

We live in a shifting world. We are going through a cultural earthquake that will profoundly affect the shape of fruitful ministry and witness in the years ahead. Understanding this earthquake will help us effectively reach the next generations.

A VIEW OF TRUTH: MODERN AND POSTMODERN

Let's look at how the modern mind of the last several centuries views truth. In modern thinking, truth is scientific and can be discovered or demonstrated by rational, analytical thought. Humans are capable of understanding and controlling the physical world. Logic, objectivity and empirical proof are effective approaches when speaking to the modern mindset.

Modern people ask questions concerning evidence for faith, proof of God's existence and God's involvement in the world. Logical, scientific and analytical approaches are very effective when speaking to a person with a modern mindset. This approach works well with scientists and engineers, for example. But many today approach knowledge and truth in a very different way.

The postmodern mindset, which is becoming more common, looks at truth as relative and situational. The physical world is ultimately beyond the control of the individual; understanding comes through relationships and community. For this mindset, effective approaches include building relationships, sharing experiences and giving personal examples of how or why something has worked.

TITANIC

The movie *Titanic* gives a stunning picture of the current shift in cultural vision. The ship represents the peak of what the modernity has made possible—an indestructible ship, a monument to the human imagination and the technological and economic capacity to triumph. The larger story is mirrored in the personal story of Rose. She is to marry the great, modern capitalist Caledon Hockley, who controls the world through an aggressive, visionary application of his reason and power. He is lord of his world, protecting his rank and privilege with all his power. Understandably, Rose is not happy.

She is trapped, suffocated by this world of power, privilege and lordly men. Jack Dawson, the artist, the man who lives for the moment, who creates his own meaning and morality, his own reality, saves Rose in "every way a person can be saved." In gripping and visually captivating drama, the ship of modernism goes down. But in the end, all that death and destruction doesn't matter. What really matters is "that the heart will go on." And so the new cultural vision, the vision of the creative artist who makes reality and lives in a world of emotional truth and relational connection, is born and baptized and even triumphs. In a poignant moment as Rose retells the story of the Titanic, she staggers to the rail of the ship she is now on and throws the most valuable diamond in the world into the sea—it's a tribute to the man who has led her into this new postmodern world and who died saving her all those decades ago. Is Jack a Christ figure for the emerging world? Is Rose's passion a model for us today? Regardless of how we respond to *Titanic,* salvation touches the core of our being.

GOD CONTINUES LOVING ALL PEOPLE!

Part of the tension we experience in the emerging culture is that God is the same yesterday, today and forever! Even in the midst of a shifting culture, God's love for all people stays the same. He was and is the God who reaches out to bring salvation. We begin our look at evangelism in the emerging culture with God's steadfast compassion.

B. IMPLICATIONS FOR WITNESS (10-15 MINUTES)*

LEADER'S NOTE

The following points give an overview of the changes in emphasis that need to take place as we witness in an emerging culture context.

Click once to advance to the next point.

MODERN	EMERGING
Great Commission	*Great Commandment*

The Great Commission as a biblical mandate resonated in modern culture. The Great Commission is centered on *truth* (teaching) and *self* (disciples). However, a new mandate may be needed in the emerging culture, possibly the Great Commandment. The Great Commandment focuses on *relationships* (neighbor and community).

Belief	*Belong*

In the modern culture, with its emphasis on intellectual truth, belief was the main point in witness. People wanted something to believe in. Now, people have a deep desire to belong. A community to belong to is a crucial starting point in witness in the emerging culture.

Present Truth	*Eternal Hope*

In the recent past, people were concerned that what they believed had to be reasonable for the here and now. In the emerging culture, people are more concerned with issues of faith that can help them through their present confusion or suffering. They need to have future hope in the midst of an unsettling present or uncertain future.

Classical Apologetics *Embodied Apologetics*

When people believed in universal truth, there was a need to demonstrate truth to those who were intellectually skeptical. Classical apologetics, an intellectual defense of the gospel, was crucial. However, in a culture that does not believe in universal truth, it is more crucial to embody the gospel in our lives. People need to see Christians "walk the walk" not just "talk the talk."

Intellectual Assent *Call to Commitment*

In modern culture we too often settled for people making a decision or intellectual assent to the Christian faith. Their lives showed very little change before they became Christians. The good news today is that as people in the emerging culture consider becoming Christians, they aren't interested in a half-way commitment. They want to be totally committed to Jesus or not committed at all. So we should call them to commitment, not decision.

C. BECKY PIPPERT INTERVIEW (10-15 MINUTES) 4

Becky Pippert has been one of the church's leaders in evangelism for the last twenty-five years. During this time Becky has seen how cultural change has affected evangelistic strategy.

Group Discussion 5

LEADER'S NOTE

Three questions are included within slide 5.

Click once to advance to the next question.

- How is evangelism in the emerging culture similar to evangelism in the modern culture?

- How has evangelism changed (or how does it need to change) as we transition to a postmodern culture?

- What draws you to the lost people in this emerging culture?

D. SCRIPTURE STUDY (30-40 MINUTES)

Before we begin to think about how to do evangelism with postmodern people, we need to grasp God's passionate concern for those who are lost. The following Bible study gives a glimpse of how Jesus thought about his own priorities.

This Bible study focuses on three related parables in Luke 15: the lost sheep (vv. 4-7), the lost coin (vv. 8-10) and the lost son (vv. 11-32).

This study is designed to paint a picture of why we should witness to others—to seek the lost. It answers the following questions:

- What is the result of finding something that is lost?
- What is the scope of this result?
- What can we learn about God's passion for the lost? How does that influence our reasons and desire to find the lost?
- How are we supposed to receive the lost when they are found?

INTRODUCING THE BIBLE STUDY*

How strong is your heartbeat for the lost, and how is that reflected in the way you spend your time, talent and resources? In Luke 15, Jesus is criticized for the way he spends his time. He is particularly criticized for the type of people he hangs out with. He answers his critics with a series of short stories. What can we learn from these three stories?

Luke 15:1-32*

Now all the tax collectors and sinners were coming near to listen to him. [2]And the Pharisees and the scribes were grumbling and saying, "This fellow welcomes sinners and eats with them."

Commentary

Verses 1-2
The Pharisees were questioning why Jesus would voluntarily associate with and even seek out sinners. These parables are his answer to their accusations.

The Lost Sheep

[3]So he told them this parable: [4]"Which one of you, having a hundred sheep and losing one of them, does not leave the ninety-nine in the wilderness and go after the one that is lost until he finds it? [5]When he has found it, he lays it on his shoulders and rejoices. [6]And when he comes home, he calls together his friends and neighbors, saying to them, 'Rejoice with me, for I have found my sheep that was lost.' [7]Just so, I tell you, there will be more joy in heaven over one sinner who

One sheep isn't that valuable. One hundred sheep indicates that the shepherd is rather wealthy. Financially, the loss of one sheep will not greatly affect him; he still has ninety-nine. But it is not a matter of the cash value of the sheep; to this shepherd every sheep is important.

The Lost Sheep (continued)

repents than over ninety-nine righteous persons who need no repentance.

Commentary

Reason for Celebration
The shepherd finds reason to celebrate in finding one sheep. In fact, it's such a powerful reason he invites all his neighbors to share his joy. The prospect of this joy is exactly why Jesus chose to associate with sinners.

The Lost Coin

8“Or what woman having ten silver coins, if she loses
one of them, does not light a lamp, sweep the house,
and search carefully until she finds it? 9When she has
found it, she calls together her friends and neighbors,
saying, ‘Rejoice with me, for I have found the coin that
I had lost.’ 10Just so, I tell you, there is joy in the
presence of the angels of God over one sinner who
repents.”

It's likely these coins were each worth about one day's wage. In this story there is monetary value to the lost item, an inherent value. While the woman probably could have survived without that one day's wage, she felt she did not have the option of not finding the coin.

Light a Lamp
This woman had to light a lamp for her search. Most likely this indicates that she lived in a small house with little light. She put forth every effort to find that one coin.

Rejoice with Me
Again, the woman was so excited to have found her missing coin that she told all her neighbors. She wanted to share her joy with others, just as God wants to share with us the joy that he has over every sinner who repents.

The Lost Son

11Then Jesus said, “There was a man who had two
sons. 12The younger of them said to his father, ‘Father,
give me the share of the property that will belong to
me.’ So he divided his property between them. 13A few
days later the younger son gathered all he had and
traveled to a distant country, and there he squandered
his property in dissolute living. 14When he had spent
everything, a severe famine took place throughout
that country, and he began to be in need. 15So he went
and hired himself out to one of the citizens of that
country, who sent him to his fields to feed the pigs.
16He would gladly have filled himself with the pods
that the pigs were eating; and no one gave him
anything. 17But when he came to himself he said, ‘How
many of my father's hired hands have bread enough
and to spare, but here I am dying of hunger! 18I will get
up and go to my father, and I will say to him, “Father,

Commentary

Give Me My Share
Inheritances were divided before the father's death only on very rare occasions. In effect, the son is saying he wishes his father were dead. The son is completely rejecting his father, willfully turning away.

He Came to His Senses
The lost son basically “finds” himself here. He realizes his mistakes, repents and chooses to return because of his circumstances. But he isn't completely “found” until his father responds to these realizations.

Welcomed with Open Arms
The father does not really listen to the

The Lost Son (continued)

I have sinned against heaven and before you; [19]I am no
longer worthy to be called your son; treat me like one
of your hired hands."' [20]So he set off and went to his
father. But while he was still far off, his father saw him
and was filled with compassion; he ran and put his
arms around him and kissed him. [21]Then the son said
to him, 'Father, I have sinned against heaven and
before you; I am no longer worthy to be called your
son.' [22]But the father said to his slaves, 'Quickly, bring
out a robe—the best one—and put it on him; put a
ring on his finger and sandals on his feet. [23]And get the
fatted calf and kill it, and let us eat and celebrate; [24]for
this son of mine was dead and is alive again; he was
lost and is found!' And they began to celebrate.
[25]"Now his elder son was in the field; and when he
came and approached the house, he heard music and
dancing. [26]He called one of the slaves and asked
whatwas going on. [27]He replied, 'Your brother has
come, and your father has killed the fatted calf,
because he has got him back safe and sound.' [28]Then
he became angry and refused to go in. His father came
out and began to plead with him. [29]But he answered
his father, 'Listen! For all these years I have been
working like a slave for you, and I have never
disobeyed your command; yet you have never given
me even a young goat so that I might celebrate with
my friends. [30]But when this son of yours came back,
who has devoured your property with prostitutes, you
killed the fatted calf for him!' [31]Then the father said to
him, 'Son, you are always with me, and all that is mine
is yours. [32]But we had to celebrate and rejoice,
because this brother of yours was dead and has come
to life; he was lost and has been found.' "

Commentary

son's speech. He has been waiting for his son to come back and immediately restores all family rights to his son. There is no partial forgiveness here, no criteria that must be met before the son can be a part of the family again. Even though the son does not expect (and certainly does not deserve) to be reinstated to the family, that is exactly what the father does. It is the same with every person who comes to faith. They are coming back to the Father, to God. They do not deserve to be made a part of his family, but that is exactly what he wants to do and what he does: full family rights and privileges, no questions asked.

Kill the Fatted Calf
Here we see the same response as in the first two parables—a major celebration. The fatted calf would have been saved for special occasions like the Day of Atonement. This is not just a welcome-home party with balloons and streamers but a major celebration—Times Square on New Year's Eve.

We Had to Celebrate
True mercy and grace includes completely accepting the lost son back into the family. This acceptance should even be embraced by his older brother. The reconciliation of today's lost person includes not only being accepted by God but also by the community around that individual.

OBSERVATION QUESTIONS*

7

1. Compare and contrast the three different parables. What are the similarities and differences?

2. What reactions do the people have to finding what they had lost?

3. What is the pattern that repeats throughout these parables?

4. Who rejoices in these parables?

Interpretation Questions* 

1. Why did Jesus tell these stories to the Pharisees? How would these stories have sounded to the Pharisees?

2. In each case, what makes the lost item valuable?

3. What do these parables communicate about how God feels about people who are lost?

4. Why doesn't the father go looking for his son? Who does the father represent?

5. What can we learn from the older brother's anger and the father's response to him?

Summarizing the Luke 15 Bible Study

This series of stories comes in a specific context. The religious people think Jesus should not be hanging out with all of these sinners, all these lost people. Jesus is a religious teacher, after all. He should hang out with religious people.

Jesus makes a captivating reply. He talks about normal stuff: a sheep, a coin, a son. And he weaves several themes through his response. Something or someone has been lost. A sheep. A coin. A son. What is lost is very valuable to the person who has lost it. That person engages in an all-out search. The shepherd hikes the hills far and wide searching for his lost sheep. The woman turns her house upside down searching for her lost coin. The father anxiously waits and watches, knowing the search will be futile until the son wants to return. When the lost is found, there is an all-out, over-the-top kind of party. The shepherd, the woman and the father can't keep their joy to themselves. Everybody is invited to share in the celebration—whether they want to or not.

Comparing the Three Parables 9

	Value	Status	Method	Result
Sheep	small worth	wealthy	long walk	rejoice
Coin	day's wage	poor	cleaning	rejoice
Son	great worth	wealthy	waiting	rejoice

All the stories share three things: something is lost, the same thing is found, the discovery brings joy. Beyond this, almost everything else is different. The characters come from different financial situations. The items have different values. The method of finding what is lost is different. Putting both the similarities and differences together is what creates the most complete picture here. Lost people, no matter what their apparent value, are very important to God, and he will search for them.

The method may be different for each person who comes to faith. One may need to hear your story; another may need to see Christ through you; yet another may come with specific questions or have nearly figured it out and just needs one last piece to make the decision. Regardless of the method there will be much rejoicing over that one person's decision to follow Christ. We should associate with those who aren't Christians in anticipation of that joy just as Jesus did (Luke 15:2).

The lost are important to God. In each parable the item that is lost—sheep, coin and son—is important to the person who lost it. It doesn't matter if it is one out of a hundred. By its mere existence, the item is important. So are sinners to God. All people, regardless of their state or apparent value in this world, are important to God.

Rejoice with me. Each seeker, on regaining what was lost, threw a party. Heaven rejoices at every sinner who repents. When those who didn't know Christ finally receive him, it is a big deal. Not only does God rejoice but so do all his angels, and so should those of us who know the person who has come to faith.

Catch the excitement. Jesus told these parables to explain why he chose to associate with sinners, directly countering the Pharisees' accusations in verse 2. The Pharisees assume it is undesirable, even wrong, to associate with sinners, but Christ's point is that it is acceptable, good and right to associate with such people. How else are they going to encounter any reason or have any desire to change? Each of the people Jesus associated with was important to him, and when one of them chose to follow him, it was reason for great joy.

The other reason for telling the parables is to motivate us by the same desires. We too should pursue the lost around us, not in an intimidating way but with love and compassion. The father in the third parable did not run after his son but waited patiently for him to return. When the son returned, the father was there for him, and he accepted his son into the family without any words about the past.

The challenge today.* Religious people tend to create programs and ministries that meet the needs of other religious people. Jesus knew that. He chose a different way. At a great cost, he chose to find the lost, to heal the sick, to cure the sinner. He wants his church to fulfill his ministry and embrace his priorities.

Lost people matter to God. God is on an all-out search to find them, and he wants partners in the search. Will you and I become partners with God to share his heart and reach the lost?

APPLICATION QUESTIONS* 10

1. How do I respond to lost people in general?

2. How do I respond to lost people in this emerging culture?

3. What changes do I need to make in how I respond to lost people today?

E. DANIEL HILL INTERVIEW (15 MINUTES)

LEADER'S NOTE

This video is a nice bridge from the Bible study to practical issues related to reaching postmodern people. Daniel clearly is excited about evangelism, but his experiences at Starbucks taught him some unexpected things about people. After showing the video, use the following questions to help the group think about people they can reach.

Group Discussion: Hill Interview

1. What surprised Daniel about the people he worked with at Starbucks?

2. What stops postmodern people from coming to God?

3. What has changed in the way modern and emerging generations view God and Christianity?

4. How do we get people to open up to God?

5. To what group of people might God be leading us to spend time with?

F. QUESTIONS OF AND RESPONSES TO MODERN AND EMERGING PEOPLE (15-20 MINUTES)*

The questions of modern and emerging people are very different. Thus the responses to the questions are also very different. It is very important to understand those differences. Moderns tend to need explanations. Emerging people are much more experiential.

Questions of Modern People

- Does God exist?
- Are miracles possible?
- Is there evidence for Jesus' resurrection?
- If God is good, loving and powerful, why is there so much evil and suffering in the world?

RESPONDING TO MODERN PEOPLE 14

EXPLANATION-ORIENTED PEOPLE

- may or may not believe in the existence of God
- want evidence, information and logical proof
- need time to explore the facts and think it through for themselves
- respond to clear and persuasive reasons for accepting Christianity
- do not like emotional appeals or powerful experiences

QUESTIONS OF EMERGING PEOPLE

LEADER'S NOTE

This section covers four specific areas where the modern and postmodern mindsets differ. Each of these principles helps us understand what postmodern people may need to move forward on their spiritual journey.

- If Christian faith works for you, what makes you think it will work for me?
- Where was God when I was suffering and in pain growing up?
- Why are Christians and the Bible so narrow, dogmatic and judgmental?
- Why is the Bible against things like premarital sex?
- In a world so diverse, how can there be only one way to God?

ALICIA AND LEAH VIDEO

LEADER'S NOTE

This video is an example of how we can respond to the questions of postmodern people. Alicia and Leah are both in their early twenties. They share an apartment together in the city. Alicia needed a housemate and met Leah through a friend. The two have learned to relate well, talk openly and share space together. The two spend time together only when they're at home at the same time. They both have separate groups of friends; they consider one another friends, but they are not close.

DISCUSSION QUESTIONS

- How did Alicia validate Leah's questions and doubts? How did Leah respond?

- How did Leah try to change the subject? How did Alicia respond?

- Alicia told a story about her brother's death. What similar stories could you share?

- How effective was Alicia in the conversation?

- How might you have approached the situation?

Responding to Emerging People

Responding to questions about faith today requires a shift in our thinking and behavior. Effective Christian "apologetics" requires a lifestyle of love and acceptance as well as appropriate answers.

Experience-Oriented People*

18

- generally believe in the existence of a God
- often have negative stereotypes of Christians and have trust issues with the church
- desire to be invited into a caring and trustworthy community where they can encounter God without necessarily accepting him
- want to hear about or witness personal stories of change
- see logical arguments as only opinions
- don't respond to pressure to accept God before they feel accepted by the community

G. THE SPIRITUAL JOURNEY OF EMERGING PEOPLE* (10-15 MINUTES)

19

LEADER'S NOTE

This section covers four specific areas where the modern and postmodern mindsets differ. Each of these principles helps us understand where postmodern people may need to move forward on their journey.

Each of the following points are included within slide 19.

Click once to advance to the point.

Trust Comes Before Truth

In the postmodern world, before anyone will listen to the truth we want to share, they first need to trust us. Who we are speaks much louder than what we say. If we are going to be effective witnesses, we must first develop a caring relationship with the people we want to share the truth with. They must know we care for them as real people with real hurts, not just as a project.

EXPERIENCE COMES BEFORE EXPLANATION

People today are looking for truth that is real, that resonates with their lives, their experiences and the experiences of their community. They are not as interested in logical proofs and explanations—at least not as the starting point for exploring Christianity. They want to know that we share or understand their experiences. Therefore, they are looking for communities where faith is lived out and spiritual experiences are tangible and real.

People's questions about religious issues are answered when our lives, words and feelings all line up. People are hungry for authenticity, for the chance to see and be a part of genuine experiences of community and of God. Genuine worship is helpful for evangelism because it is an authentic experience of the reality of God in community. Healing experiences, especially emotional healing, are also becoming more important. In the past, being an expert and having the answers is what built credibility. Today, credibility is based on having questions, struggles and hurts in common with others. Once people have seen authenticity in our lives, they are more ready to listen to the explanations of the faith that we offer. Whether or not an explanation has authority is based on the credibility demonstrated.

For experience-oriented people, trust is the key! Sadly, broken trust is very pervasive.

BELONGING COMES BEFORE BELIEVING

Postmodern people are looking for a safe and accepting community in which they can work out their identity. They want to belong to something that they can believe in, but they need to be a part of that community before they can determine if it is in fact worth believing in.

"I have to reinvent myself anew each day" is the feeling of many postmoderns. They want to belong to a community that will be supportive of the struggle inherent in that statement. Once they feel they belong, they will most likely come to believe what that community believes. We need to welcome people into Christian fellowship so that they can feel there is a place for them in the church. Then they will be more likely to listen to and accept the gospel.

IMAGE COMES BEFORE WORD

The battle for allegiance today is a battle for the spiritual and moral imagination of people. And imagination is caught much more easily with images than words. Words explain only after the image has been observed.

> There is now an immense interest in the university in art and its relation to truth, goodness and beauty. There is a growing commitment to art as the primary way for re-making the moral and spiritual imagination. (Willie Jennings, professor at Duke Divinity School)

Art is becoming the most compelling media of communication. To immediately and more effectively convey a message, show people an image. They may not interpret it as we intend, but it will get their attention, and they will get *something* out of it immediately. Words can be used to explain the original intent of the image if necessary. Those who know how to create and use images are the ones being listened to.

Identification Comes Before Influence

The "big story" (metanarrative) of Western social and scientific progress and dominance has been replaced by a million little stories (micronarratives) of cultural conflict and competition. People must be able to identify with our story before we will have any influence on them.

To capture the emerging culture we must first capture the storyline of the culture. People must be able to see and experience the biblical "big story" of God's multinational, multicultural kingdom of love and justice. We must also show clearly that God's story is inclusive and identifies with all the little stories people tell.

As people see that God's story is much bigger and grander than their own, yet he still identifies with their stories, they become ready to be transformed into God's people who are part of his grand story.

Conclusion

Our apologetic must be holistic and incarnational, speaking to the hearts, heads *and* hands of people. And it must involve people in an experience and explanation of Christ's presence and kingdom reality.

H. LESSONS FROM THE PAST: ROMAN VERSUS CELTIC MODEL (10-15 MINUTES)*

LEADER'S NOTE

Following the explanation of the two styles, there is a small group discussion time for participants to process the models and figure out how they can apply the lessons of this witness module to their own community.

This section looks at the Roman and Celtic models of evangelism in order to explore changes in evangelism strategy. Evangelism strategies, just like many other things in history, change from culture to culture.

Lessons from the Past 20

Often we can learn from past models how to do ministry in the present and future. Roman culture was very similar to modern culture. Celtic culture of the Middle Ages was very similar to the emerging culture. Let's see what we can learn from how the church interacted in these two cultures.

ROMAN MODEL	**CELTIC MODEL**
Persuasion Evangelism	*Incarnation Evangelism*

In the Roman model of Christian evangelism there was a strong emphasis on persuasion and reason. That method did not work in Celtic culture. For the Celts the gospel needed to be incarnated in the lives of the Christians before they would respond to the gospel.

Proclamation	*Soul Awakening*

In Roman culture the gospel was proclaimed, people heard, and they responded. In Celtic culture people were awakened to the gospel by an event.

Conversion = Decision	*Inclusion in Community*

In Roman culture people made decisions to become Christians before they entered the Christian community. In the Celtic culture people were invited to be a part of the Christian community to experience the spiritual faith before they became Christians.

Inclusion in Church	*Transformation*

After they became Christians, Roman people were welcomed into the church. In Celtic culture people were already experiencing the benefits of community before they became Christians. From within the community they were transformed to become followers of Jesus.

I. CONVERSION IN THE EMERGING CULTURE (15-20 MINUTES)

ABNER AND THE EDGE 21

LEADER'S NOTE

This video presents the story of one student's conversion experience. Not everyone's spiritual journey is the same, but Abner is a good example of a path many in the emerging culture follow. Abner's story is a good way to review the four principles just presented. Take a few minutes to draw out from the group a list of steps Abner went through.

- What do you notice in this video about Abner's conversion process?

POSTMODERN CONVERSION PROCESS* 22

The postmodern conversion process flows through the elements discussed above in "The Spiritual Journey of Emerging People." While not every person is on the same journey, we can often collaborate with and serve what God is doing in another's life by being attentive to their process.

LEADER'S NOTE

Each of the following five points and are included within slide 23.

Click once to advance to the next point.

- ***Friendship and Prayer.*** "Trust before truth" means we start by building close friendships and pray that our new friends will not only trust us but be open to God working in their lives.
- ***Soul Awakening.*** "Experience before explanation" means we not only pray that our friends will be open to God's work in their lives but also provide opportunities for them to be exposed to powerful and transforming experiences with God (e.g., vibrant worship services).
- ***Community.*** "Belonging before believing" also means we draw pre-Christians into an exploratory community where they can ask questions and experience openhearted support in their search for a sense of identity and self.
- ***Conversion.*** To help our friends become converted not just to our Christian community but to Jesus, the King of the community, we need to realize that many postmoderns need to grasp the *image* of and not just biblical *words* about the cross. For many people today "image comes before word." They need to visualize, not just hear about, what Christ accomplished on the cross.
- ***Transformation.*** As emerging people see God (and God's people) identifying with all their hurts and fears, they become increasingly open to living a transformed life.

How are you serving the postmodern conversion process with your actions?

J. WITNESS QUESTIONS (5-10 MINUTES)* 23

- In what ways will our witness need to be different in this emerging culture?
- What is the relationship between witness and community?
- What is the relationship between witness and justice?
- Where is your church strong in connecting with and reaching more experience-oriented, community-hungry, unchurched people?

ADDITIONAL EXERCISES (OPTIONAL)

ALEX AND JASON 24

This video shows how you can move a friendship into a spiritual relationship. Alex and Jason are coworkers and buddies. They don't know a lot about one another's past, but they do enjoy spending time together during work and occasionally after work. At a chance meeting in a restaurant the spiritual ideas presented in movies come up.

LEADER'S NOTE

Each of the questions below are included within slide 26.

Click once to advance to the next question.

DISCUSSION QUESTIONS

- Why was Jason able to have this conversation with Alex?
- How did Alex try to change the subject? How was Jason able to bring the conversation back to spiritual topics?
- Where and how could Jason have improved his presentation?
- How would you have responded in the situation?

ANA AND ROSA 26

This video models how Christians can have a redemptive conversation with someone struggling with homosexuality by weaving together love and truth while challenging them to the next step in a relationship with Jesus. By love we mean not being judgmental but taking seriously and identifying with their feelings and thoughts. Also being loving means not holding back on being honest and speaking the truth.

LEADER'S NOTE

Each of the questiohs below are included within slide 27.

Click once to advance to the next question.

Discussion Questions 27

- In the conversation, when did Ana or Rosa respond unexpectedly? How did the other react?

- You've probably heard the phrase "hate the sin but love the sinner." How did Ana respond in that way (or not)?

- How did these sisters' relationship affect the conversation? How might a different relationship influence the conversation?

- What types of comments seemed to be effective? What would you say or do differently?

Select Resources

The Celtic Way of Evangelism by George Hunter
Evangelism Outside the Box by Rick Richardson
"Generating Hope," in *Telling the Truth: Evangelizing Postmoderns* by Jimmy Long
Jesus for a New Generation by Kevin Ford
Out of the Saltshaker by Becky Pippert
The Power of Story by Leighton Ford

4
Communication

OVERVIEW

Introduction*

This communication module focuses on the cultural shift from a word-based communication style to an image-based communication style. We will examine the impact of this shift on Bible study, worship and preaching. Rather than choosing one over another, this module explores the biblical pattern of combining both image and word in communication.

> **Additional Materials**
> Using the imagination in Scripture study:
> - pencils, crayons, markers, chalks, finger paint, etc., to do art on paper
> - Play-Doh for sculpting
> - blank sheets of paper, magazines, scissors and glue sticks to mount collages on construction paper or poster board

Questions Covered*

- What are the inherent characteristics of words and images?
- What are the advantages and dangers of words and images in communication?
- How does the Bible use words and images in communication?
- How can images and words appropriately be used in Bible study, worship and preaching?

Content Flow

The following is a suggestion of how to arrange learning components in this module. Use the components to customize the training for your audience and time frame.

A. Introduction (10-15 minutes)

B. Words and Images (10-15 minutes)

C. Implications for Communication (10-15 minutes)

D. Scripture Study (30-40 minutes)

E. Strengths and Weaknesses of Images and Words (20-30 minutes)

F. Bible Study Changes in Emerging Culture (15-20 minutes)

G. Worship in the Emerging Culture (15-20 minutes)

H. Preaching in the Emerging Culture (15-20 minutes)

I. Communication Questions (5-10 minutes)

COMMUNICATION: WORD AND IMAGE

A. INTRODUCTION (10-15 MINUTES)

LORD OF THE RINGS 2-3

"Have you seen *The Lord of the Rings?* What did you think?" This has been one of the buzz conversations since the film version of J. R. R. Tolkien's popular novel was released as a movie. Some of Tolkien's most devoted fans have decided not to see the film, believing that there is no way a film could faithfully represent the novel. Other fans have been eager to see how the filmmakers would bring these stories to life. Some who have never read *The Lord of the Rings* trilogy are watching the film as a faster, more immediately gripping alternative to the lengthy novel. Due to an advertising blitz with glossy Tolkien displays and new editions of all of his books, people are rereading the trilogy or even reading it for the first time. *The Lord of the Rings* film raises the question, Do you watch the movie, read the book or both?

The conflict (real or imagined) between written words and visual images, particularly moving images, has been going on for years. It appears to most that images are winning. People spend far more time watching TV and movies than they do reading. Living rooms are arranged with the couches directly facing the TV. Rooms that used to be libraries are now media rooms with entertainment centers. The increasing role images play in communication is one of the marks of the emerging culture.[1] Even TV has shifted from objective word-based communication to more subjective, image-based communication. (Compare, in your mind, the two car commercials that you saw in the overview module.)

WORD AND IMAGE: BOOKS VS. TV

In one sense it is difficult for hundreds of pages of plain black text to compete with fast-moving, colorful pictures; on the other hand, images have a harder time expressing com-

---

[1]See Mitchell Stephens, *The Rise of the Image, the Fall of the Word* (Oxford University Press, 1998). In the early chapters Stephens makes the strong case for the recent ascendancy of the image.

plex or abstract ideas in a concrete way. In their own way both images and words do a good job of telling a story or eliciting emotions. Reading continues to be very highly regarded: "According to the Gallup Poll, 61% of us proclaim reading 'more rewarding' than watching television; 73% lament that we spend too little time reading books; and 92% of us attest that reading is a 'good use' of our time." Meanwhile, the television is called the "boob tube," and people who watch it are "couch potatoes," passive observers whose minds are being numbed. Several questions might be raised. If reading is so rewarding, why do we do so little of it? If images have so much potential for powerful communication, why is so much visual media shabby and debased?

THE WORD-IMAGE DILEMMA

Current circumstances present a dilemma to Bible study leaders, worship leaders and preachers and teachers of the gospel. Many traditional means of communicating the gospel (at least in the Protestant tradition) are word-based. Bible study, of course, happens mostly through books. With some exceptions, preaching is not overly visual—it usually consists of listening to someone else speak. Many teachers and preachers of the gospel feel they are presented with an unsavory choice: continue with word-based forms of communication, losing the attention of listeners who are increasingly familiar with sophisticated visual communication, or accommodate the video culture and risk "dumbing down" the gospel, reducing it to entertainment or losing its content altogether. How can preachers and teachers reach their audience with the substance of their message while remaining relevant in an image-dominated culture?

BRIDGING THE GAP BETWEEN WORDS AND IMAGES

Thankfully, we are not limited to a choice between "boring" words and "empty" images. In this training module we will explore the fact that we need not be locked into a winner-take-all battle between word and image. Perhaps the rise of the image does not necessarily mean the fall of the word; perhaps the rise of the image could open powerful new opportunities for preaching and teaching.

QUESTIONS TO BE EXAMINED

Together, we will address the following questions:

- Why are images so popular?
- Why are words so well-respected?
- What are the strengths and weaknesses of words? Of images?
- What does the Bible have to say about the relationship between words and images?
- How do we use images effectively and meaningfully in Bible study, worship and preaching?

We will look for answers through studying Scripture and examining the nature of words and images. Get ready to use your heads, hearts and eyes.

B. WORDS AND IMAGES (10-15 MINUTES)

LEADER'S NOTE

The three-minute video juxtaposes images and words. It is an overture for the issues and ideas to come. Use it to get people thinking about how images and words work differently and how they work together. After showing the video, briefly discuss it with some of the following questions.

WORD AND IMAGE VIDEO 

Video Content Overview

Caption	***Subject matter***
Take control	tech toys; cell phone, stereo, TV
Be a road warrior	Sport Utility Vehicles
You'll never be lonely again	computers; people and computers
Satisfy your self	leisure, self-indulgence
Get what's rightfully yours	physical strength/power, violence
Surrender to your passions	people kissing, passion
Get out of my way	cars
Everyone is having great sex	possession, smoldering looks
Life is easier with alcohol	party scenes, individual drinks
Diamonds are forever	jewelry
Pretty people win	women
Hide your blemishes	makeup
Parts are greater than the whole	close-ups of eyes, lips and legs
Fill the void	food

VIDEO QUESTIONS 

- What were some of your general impressions or responses?
- What did the images communicate?
- What did the words communicate?
- What are some of the differences between the words and the images?
- How did the words and images work together?

C. IMPLICATIONS FOR COMMUNICATION* (10-15 MINUTES)

7

Our communication patterns will need to change if we are going to be able to communicate with people who are becoming more and more influenced by the emerging culture. Are we willing to adopt new communication patterns? Let's look at some of the changes that might need to be made.

LEADER'S NOTE

The implications are included within slide 7.

Click to advance through the implications one by one.

MODERN	EMERGING
Word	*Image*

As we have already seen, image has become a powerful tool within our culture. Our first response is usually that this is a negative change. However, God continually uses images to communicate with us. We need to be sure we use both word and image in our communication so we can connect with all the God-given senses each person possesses.

Detached *Participant*

In modern culture we were taught to be objective and to remain detached from what we were studying. We were taught to use our mind and check the passions of our heart. Today, however, while we still need to use our mind, we also recognize that none of us can be totally objective. We bring our own past understanding and experience, and thus should feel free to fully participate in the learning experience with both our mind and heart.

Didactic *Narrative*

Just as modernity taught us to be objective and detached, it also taught us that the didactic (teaching) portions of Scripture were preferred to stories or narrative portions. However, we are now discovering that Scripture is one big narrative of God's kingdom story. The Scripture, our spiritual lives and our learning experience need to be couched within the narrative of God's larger story.

Knowledge *Transformation*

In the past we too often thought that the goal of communication was more knowledge. If we had more knowledge in our minds, we would use that knowledge for good. However, we have seen that knowledge by itself is not enough. Through the emerging culture, Christians are being reminded that the true goal is not more knowledge but transformation. We need our hearts changed, not just our minds filled.

Inward-focused *Mission-focused*

Communication in the latter part of the modern culture often centered on the individual, on ourselves. What's in it for me? was the question most frequently asked. But people in the emerging culture are not so self-centered; their focus is on the community. Hopefully, Christians will be reminded that the universe does not center around us but on God and what he wants to accomplish in and through us in the surrounding communities.

D. SCRIPTURE STUDY (30-40 MINUTES)* 8

This Bible study compares two passages: Exodus 3:1-10 and Exodus 32:1-8. The first passage is the story of God's call to Moses through the burning bush. In the second passage the Hebrew people become impatient waiting for Moses, who is on the mountain, so they make a golden calf to worship.

The first passage describes encounters between God and people, in which God uses both pictures and words to communicate. The second passage tells the story about having a false "picture" of God. The Hebrews do not want to see the real God, and yet they make an image of God in direct disobedience to the words God has just spoken to them.

Together these passages give us an initial understanding of the place of words and images. As you read the Scripture, keep these questions in mind:

- How does God use words and images in these passages?
- Is there a relationship between the two?
- Why do people make false images?
- How do the false images compare to true ones?
- In what ways are images and words dangerous?

LEADER'S NOTE

An annotated version of the Scripture study follows with some notes to help you prepare.

Exodus 3:1-10

Moses was keeping the flock of his father-in-law Jethro,
the priest of Midian; he led his flock beyond the
wilderness, and came to Horeb, the mountain of God.
[2]There the angel of the LORD appeared to him in a flame
of fire out of a bush; he looked, and the bush was
blazing, yet it was not consumed. [3]Then Moses said, "I
must turn aside and look at this great sight, and see
why the bush is not burned up." [4]When the LORD saw
that he had turned aside to see, God called to him out
of the bush, "Moses, Moses!" And he said, "Here I am."
[5]Then he said, "Come no closer! Remove the sandals
from your feet, for the place on which you are standing
is holy ground." [6]He said further, "I am the God of your
father, the God of Abraham, the God of Isaac, and the
God of Jacob." And Moses hid his face, for he was afraid
to look at God.

Commentary

God uses an image to draw Moses from his normal path. Images open up new possibilities for us. The most important phrase in this passage is verse 3, "I must turn aside and look at this great sight." First the eye is caught; then the eye is engaged. Moses' response to the image is initially curiosity and excitement, then fear when words tell him that he is in the presence of God.

Exodus 3:1-10 ***(continued)***

7 Then the LORD said, "I have observed the misery of my
people who are in Egypt; I have heard their cry on
account of their taskmasters. Indeed, I know their
sufferings, 8 and I have come down to deliver them from
the Egyptians, and to bring them up out of that land to
a good and broad land, a land flowing with milk and
honey, to the country of the Canaanites, the Hittites,
the Amorites, the Perizzites, the Hivites, and the
Jebusites. 9 The cry of the Israelites has now come to
me; I have also seen how the Egyptians oppress them.
10 So come, I will send you to Pharaoh to bring my
people, the Israelites, out of Egypt."

Commentary

The encounter with the image prepares him for the word. Even with this image, God's words end up being a tough sell for Moses. What would it have been like without the burning bush? God could have just spoken to Moses to get his attention, but he wouldn't have been as ready to receive the word. The image puts him into the proper frame of mind to receive the word.

Exodus 32:1-8

When the people saw that Moses delayed to come down
from the mountain, the people gathered around Aaron,
and said to him, "Come, make gods for us, who shall go
before us; as for this Moses, the man who brought us up
out of the land of Egypt, we do not know what has
become of him." 2 Aaron said to them, "Take off the gold
rings that are on the ears of your wives, your sons, and
your daughters, and bring them to me." 3 So all the
people took off the gold rings from their ears, and
brought them to Aaron. 4 He took the gold from them,
formed it in a mold, and cast an image of a calf; and they
said, "These are your gods, O Israel, who brought you
up out of the land of Egypt!" 5 When Aaron saw this, he
built an altar before it; and Aaron made proclamation
and said, "Tomorrow shall be a festival to the LORD."
6 They rose early the next day, and offered burnt
offerings and brought sacrifices of well-being; and the
people sat down to eat and drink, and rose up to revel.
7 The LORD said to Moses, "Go down at once! Your
people, whom you brought up out of the land of Egypt,
have acted perversely; 8 they have been quick to turn
aside from the way that I commanded them; they have
cast for themselves an image of a calf, and have
worshiped it and sacrificed to it, and said, 'These are
your gods, O Israel, who brought you up out of the
land of Egypt!' "

The Israelites fear the God-given image. Rather than asking God to manifest himself visually, they made their own image. This false image not only was self-made, but it was a direct rejection of the God-given image.

They are attracted to the safety of the false image. They know it won't kill them. The golden calf is a more explicable image than the one God gives them—it's tame, domestic and easy to comprehend. It's at their beck and call.

The creation of this idol seems to come out of a desire to make God's images less intense. The burning bush elicits attraction and awe. It is an intense, overwhelming sensory experience. The golden calf is beautiful, but not overwhelming; attractive, but not awesome.

The Israelites' response to the calf is pitiful. Their worship lacks the awe that was present in their response to God's appearances.

One of the lessons of the golden calf is that our eyes are unsatisfied without an image—if we are not looking at an image of God, we will make something else that catches our eye and worship that instead.

OBSERVATION QUESTIONS*

1. Compare and contrast the two stories. What are the similarities and differences?

2. Where do you see the use of words and images in the passages?

3. How do people respond to the words and the images in these passages?

4. What communication patterns do you see?

5. Compare and contrast God's own image with the Israelites' false image.

Interpretation Questions* 10

1. What about the burning bush causes Moses to stop?

2. What do these passages tell you about God? About people?

3. Why does God use both words and images? Why not just one or the other?

4. How are the words and images related to one another?

5. Why do the Hebrews prefer the golden calf?

Summary of the Exodus Study 11

LEADER'S NOTE

The main points below are included within slide 11.

Click once to advance to each question.

God Reveals Himself in Images and Words

One striking feature of these passages is that God chooses to use images to communicate with his people. It is easy to assume that to be Word-based requires the exclusive use of words. After all, our most common experience of God's revelation comes from reading words in the Bible. It is easy to forget, though, that what we are reading about is often a multisensory experience of the revelation of God.

In the first passage God chooses to reveal himself in both image and word. In Exodus 3:1-10 the image appears first. The meaning of this image is not entirely clear and never explained; we do not know why God chose to appear through a burning bush. While a precise interpretation of the image is not available, its effect is quite clear. The image commands attention and evokes awe.

God's Images Catch Attention, His Words Give Direction

Essentially, the image says, "Pay attention! Something very important is about to be said."

It's as if God doesn't want to have to shout over the hubbub, so he uses images to quiet the crowd. In contrast to images, the meaning of the words is very clear and direct. The words give Moses and the people of Israel new directions for their life: Moses is given the mission to rescue the Hebrews. The image calls Moses to "turn aside" from his current path; the words give Moses and the Hebrews directions to a new destination.

FALSE IMAGES ARE DANGEROUS

The second passage shows that the attractive quality of images is not always a good thing. Through images, humans can be pulled off as easily as drawn toward the right path. In Exodus 32 the people of Israel "turn aside" toward an image. Unfortunately, they turn aside from worshiping God in order to worship a false image.

The story of the golden calf serves as a warning. Images are powerful tools. We have to be careful about what we focus our eyes on. As Jesus says in Luke 11:34, "If your eye is healthy, your whole body is full of light; but if it is not healthy, your body is full of darkness." It's hard to turn your eye somewhere without your whole body following. The Israelites don't want to see the image of the stormy mountain. They ask God to take that image away, and soon their eyes start to wander. They create a new image for their eyes, and they worship it.

It's important to notice that the false image does not bear full responsibility. False words play their part. God's words command them not to make or worship idols; he also commands them not to take his name in vain or bear false witness (see Exodus 20). They do all these things in making an idol, justifying their actions afterward. False images and false words tend to go together.

As we try to recognize false images and true images, it is helpful to note that the image of the golden calf lacks all of the wildness of the burning bush. It seems that God prefers images that overwhelm our senses and understanding. When we make our own (false) images, we tend to make them more comfortable.

E. STRENGTHS AND WEAKNESSES OF IMAGES AND WORDS (20-30 MINUTES)

LEADER'S NOTE

This segment is a follow-up to the burning bush and golden calf passages, and offers observations about the nature of words and images. It will recap ideas from the Bible study and then explore ideas already mentioned while adding some new ones. You may want to add your own examples as illustrations.

In God's interaction with Moses and the Israelites, he uses both words and images. It would be difficult to imagine his message being as clear and compelling if he used only one or the other. As we have seen in the Scripture study, both forms of communication have unique advantages and disadvantages. Words or images can effectively express many ideas; on the other hand, it's possible to be ineffective with either form of communication. How should we then understand word- and image-based communication in the emerging culture?

FOCUS* 12

Images—attract the eye

[NEON CROSS] 13

Words—discipline our thoughts 14

LEADER'S NOTE

The Hebrews text is included within slide 14.

Click once to call it up.

> HEBREWS 12:2
> Let us fix our eyes on Jesus, the author and perfecter of our faith, who for the joy set before him endured the cross, scorning its shame, and sat down at the right hand of the throne of God.

Images and words have different capacities for focusing our attention. As we saw in the story of the burning bush~~, images have a unique~~ ability to turn the head—to change the direction of the focus. Although this is true of still images, it is particularly so with moving ones.

LEADER'S NOTE

At this point advance to the next PowerPoint slide (a moving image) and keep talking. 15
After a few moments you can stop and ask the audience where their attention has been.

In fact, experts tell us that it is almost impossible for us not to look at moving images. Several years ago research by Harvard professor Rudolf Arnheim explained how the human eye is drawn to motion as a defense mechanism.[2] Our eyes automatically make

---

[2]Rudolf Arnheim, *Visual Thinking* (University of California Press, 1969), p. 165. Arnheim's book is a classic in the field of visual communication. He has helpful insights about many aspects about words and images. See also Stephens, *Rise of the Image,* p.165. Stephens tells the story of doing a classroom experiment much like the experiment proposed here. In Stephens's situation after a few minutes even the most skeptical student realized the pull of moving images.

quick glances toward any changing spot to determine its importance to us personally. Moving images draw our attention.

Whereas images have the ability to change our field of vision, words focus our attention by improving clarity. Images have a more difficult time than words in creating clear categories for thinking. It's these clear categories that provide the proper environment for sustained argument. While images turn the head, words facilitate closer consideration of and deliberation about a subject.

DESCRIPTION*

Images—describe surfaces and appearances 16-17

Words—capture abstract ideas and thoughts 18-19

"The view from here was orchards: pecan, plum, apple. The highway ran along the river, dividing the orchards like a long, crooked part in a leafy scalp. The trees filled the whole valley floor to the sides of the canyon. Confetti-colored houses perched on the slopes at its edges with their backs to the canyon wall. And up at the head of the canyon was the old Black Mountain copper mine. On the cliff overlooking the valley, the smelter's one brick smokestack pointed obscenely at the heavens." Barbara Kingsolver, *Animal Dreams* (Harper Collins, 1990), p. 9.

Words and Images—elicit emotions and feelings 20

Both words and images are excellent communication tools. However, depending on the subject, each has a strong advantage over the other. The advantage of images is in representing physical appearances. This ability is the foundation of the phrase "A picture is worth a thousand words." One can certainly describe physical attributes with words, but much less precisely or concisely.

On the other hand, while images can connect powerfully to our emotions, they cannot describe or examine the inner world of mind and heart the way words can. Even films have a hard time with "subtler mental states."

Films are capable of dazzling physical representations, but in presenting motivations and lines of thought, they cannot compare with novels.

Images—simultaneous

One area in which images have an almost absolute advantage is in simultaneous presentation of multiple items. It is simply impossible for words to describe more than one thing at a time. Images, however, quite easily show different objects in spatial relation to one another.

[TABLE WITH SOUP] 21

Words—sequential 22

It is, of course, possible for words to describe more than one thing and how they relate to one another. Words, however, cannot do so as immediately as images can. Words require more of a step-by-step process: "A successful literary image grows through what one might call accretion by amendment. Each word, each statement, is amended by the next into something closer to the intended total meaning."[3]

However, even with this limitation words can be used effectively. Because of this step-by-step process, words can precisely control the building of an image. Words allow the describer to edit based on the significance of the details rather than simply on mere spatial relationships. Arnheim says, "The description of the scene becomes an interpretation."[4] This sort of arrangement can be done in only a limited fashion with still images. It is, however, quite possible to do it as well with moving images, especially when cutting and multiple camera angles are used.

Images—concrete and specific 23-24

With the notable exception of abstract art, images portray specific objects. An image shows a particular tree; it cannot very easily describe the concept of a tree.

Words—abstract and general 

While words cannot portray the particular tree nearly as easily as the image can, words can discuss trees in general far more easily.

LEADER'S NOTE

The word "Tree" is included in slide 25. It will appear after a short pause.

INTERPRETATION*

Images—multiplicity of meanings 26-27

Whereas images can depict an object very precisely, they often have a difficult time communicating the meaning of the object. This difficulty is largely due to a multiplicity of possible meanings without enough information to choose from. Aquinas gives one example of the problem: "For instance the lion may mean the Lord because of one similitude and the Devil because of another."[5]

Stephens goes on to say, "We are not born with, nor have we created, any particularly sophisticated systems for organizing still images to specify or build meanings."[6]

Words—narrow the potential meanings 28

---

[3]Arnheim, *Visual Thinking,* p. 249.
[4]Ibid., p. 248.
[5]Quoted in Stephens, *Rise of the Image,* p. 66.
[6]Ibid., p. 68.

LEADER'S NOTE

Three examples of narrowing meanings are included in slide 28. All three will appear after a short pause.

We do, however, have such a system for words. The rules of grammar, the fact that we can form sentences and paragraphs to qualify our statements, allow us to successfully narrow the range of potential meanings of our words.

Images Without Words—vague or cliché 29-30

When images are not combined with words, they often offer no meaning or are clear but dull. Anyone who has played charades has witnessed both of these tendencies. Often, the actor reverts to stereotyped symbols for quick responses. Just as frequently, those who are guessing flail wildly in their attempts to interpret a vague gesture.

Words Without Images—abstract 31

Words without images simply tend toward too great a degree of abstraction. An example of this abstraction is found in 1 Corinthians 1:18. In fact, studies of sensory deprivation show that without sensory input we tend to lose the ability to think cogently.[7]

This is probably because much of our vocabulary, even at the most conceptual level, is based on metaphors of physical perception. For instance, we describe thoughts that are particularly thoughtful as "deep." Images supply the raw material for the ideas behind words.

LEADER'S NOTE

1 Corinthians 1:18 is included in slide 31.

Click once to make the passage appear.

TEMPTATION*

Images—bend toward idolatry 32-33

We have focused mostly on the different positive capabilities of words and images. But both forms of communication are susceptible to abuse. We see the sinful tendency of images in the golden calf: images can become idols.

Words—bend toward lies 34-35

Words present a different temptation. Words can be twisted to form lies. Images show

---

[7]Arnheim, *Visual Thinking*, p. 19.

the surfaces of things and remain open to a multiplicity of interpretations, thus they entrance but do not deceive easily. Words, on the other hand, draw a person along their own path of logic, thus they can lead us into unwitting error.

We must be on the lookout for both false images and false words. We must be open to true images that present God and our life situation in ways that words by themselves cannot.

Application of Word and Image 36

So far we have primarily focused on understanding how word and image relate to each other in the abstract. Now let's try to understand how both word and image should shape how we do Bible study, worship, preaching and teaching.

LEADER'S NOTE

The three application points below are included in slide 36.

Click once for each of the three points.

Bible Study
Worship
Preaching or Teaching

F. BIBLE STUDY CHANGES IN EMERGING CULTURE (15-20 MINUTES)* 37

Whether we realize it or not, our Bible study methods were greatly influenced by modernism. Many of those influences were very positive. However, some were not as positive. As we continue moving into the emerging culture, we need to take corrective measures so our Bible study can be what God intended it to be.

LEADER'S NOTE

The following points are included in slide 37.

Click once for each point under the "Modern" column and then for the "Emerging" column.

Modern	Emerging
Detached Observer	*Avid Participant*

To remain objective, we were taught in the past to approach Scripture as a detached observer. However, the Scriptures were mostly written in the midst of specific circumstances, often in the midst of serious crisis situations. To fully appreciate Scripture, we cannot remain detached but need to be involved as participants.

Discover Truth *Encounter Jesus*

Since modern culture is knowledge-based, the goal of learning is more knowledge. Thus in Scripture study the goal was discovering more truth. However, more knowledge or more truth does not always bring about changed lives. In the emerging culture we need to think and act more relationally. So instead of merely gaining more truth, our goal should be to encounter Jesus and let him transform our whole being, not just our mind.

Individually *Communally*

Our primary means of Bible study and application in the past was centered on the individual. Today, though, we are relearning that we were created to live in community. That community should spill over into our Bible study and application. God has given spiritual gifts to each of us that we might learn from each other.

Right Answers *Good Questions*

Before, we were primarily concerned with finding the right answers. To accomplish that task we sometimes did not take seriously the context of the biblical situation. We were proof texting, looking for verses that backed up what we already believed. But to really find the right answers, we need to start with good questions that allow us to understand the context of the situation.

Study a Passage *Enter the Text*

In modern culture we were called to *study* a passage (using primarily our mind), but we were not *entering* the text (using all of our senses). Now, in order for people to see the relevance of the text, they need to actively identify with the people or concepts involved in the text, not just passively study the passage.

Leader as Teacher *Leader as Learner*

In the past, church leaders were seen as Bible experts who could dispense biblical information to others. Today's leaders need to recognize that knowledge is only one of the means to the goal of transformation. We all need to consider ourselves as learners because God is continually transforming all of us into the image of Jesus.

EMERGING CULTURE COMMUNAL BIBLE STUDY

Goal for Communal Bible Study* 38

"Our goal for the Bible study is for the participants to encounter Jesus. This means that they not only learn the truth about Jesus as shown in the Scripture, but also experience the presence of Jesus in every element of their time gathered as a small group, from the hospitality of the leader, to the gentle and loving interaction with the other members, to how well they are listened." Lindsey Olesberg, InterVarsity's National Bible Study Coordinator

Here is an example of what a communal Bible study might look like. This type of study is more appropriate for people living in this emerging culture. The minutes indicated are suggested breakdowns for a forty-five minute Bible study.

LEADER'S NOTE

The following six points are included in slide 39.

Click once for each point.

INTRODUCTION (2 MINUTES) 39

More people today have a limited understanding of biblical backgrounds. Therefore, we need to make sure they understand the biblical context and pertinent background information needed for the study. They also will need to have some understanding of how this study might connect to today's context.

ENTER THE TEXT (10 MINUTES)

In the past we tried to study Scripture "detached" from our personal situation. Today people need to be more involved. We need to give them an exercise at the beginning of our study that will encourage them to interact with the text by using different senses. After reading the passage, have them do one of the following:

- Describe how you would have felt if you were there.
- Draw a picture that presents the situation.
- Describe how the different characters would feel.
- Put the Scripture into your own words.

DEVELOP QUESTIONS (5-10 MINUTES)

As a group, reread the passage and have everyone write down what they think are the key questions that need to be discussed for the group to understand what the passage says and means. Have everyone share the questions they wrote down. This exercise will make sure the whole group has a say in what is essential for them to understand the passage. As the leader, arrange the key questions in some type of order. (Hopefully, you have done your own study beforehand so you can anticipate some of the key questions.)

ANSWER QUESTIONS TOGETHER (10-15 MINUTES)

Using the order you developed above, have the group proceed to answer the questions. Feel free to pursue a given theme from the passage through to its application; you don't have to wait to the end of the study to do the application.

SUMMARIZE (3 MINUTES)

As the leader, summarize the context of the passage, your understanding of the passage and how the passage fits into the larger picture of God's kingdom story. (Here is your opportunity to do some teaching.)

APPLICATION (10 MINUTES)

If you haven't discussed the application of the Scripture to your group's situation, do so now. Application can be focused on the individual or the group, inward or outward. But remember that in the past most application centered on the individual and was inward focused. In the emerging culture we need to be less focused on ourselves and our desires and more focused on the community and on what God is doing.

ENTERING THE TEXT EXERCISE (OPTIONAL)*

LEADER'S NOTE

This segment is an opportunity to practice working with images and the imagination in Scripture study. In this segment, most of the time is spent doing the creativity exercise below; make sure you obtain the necessary materials beforehand.

Break into small groups of three to four. Assign a portion of the Exodus Scriptures we looked at earlier to each person. Let them read the passage again and tap into their imagination. Ask: What images do you see in your mind's eye? Can you capture it in a drawing? A poem? Something else? Let's take the next ten minutes to think and create. Give the group ten minutes to work, less time if it seems people are getting restless or have completed the exercise.

Then give the group members two to three minutes to share their work. Remind them not to criticize, analyze too deeply or share for too long! At the conclusion debrief the whole group by asking what they learned.

Exercise Introduction

We've spent some time observing the way God has used images in Scripture to communicate, and we've noted the different strengths of words and images. Now it's time for us to think about how to effectively use images with words in our own communication.

Activate the Imagination!

Using images in communication is not simply a matter of using visual aids. Visual aids don't always activate the imagination, and the imagination can be activated without visual aids. Our goal is *not* to make our sermons and Bible studies simply more entertaining, but to draw out the power of the image in the Word of God by awakening a biblical imagination. Often the power of imagery in Scripture goes untapped, and we get a lopsided experience of God's revelation. Images are powerful because they access the imagination by *grabbing our attention, provoking curiosity* and *pulling us further into* interaction with God.

As you work at awakening the imagination in Scripture study, try starting your Bible study with an imagination exercise. Most of the time with Bible study, we are aiming for a participatory atmosphere, and using images is a great way to enhance group dynamics and get people engaged in the passage. Using our imagination gets us deeper into the Word, helping us to interact creatively with the text and with one another.

The Goal
Use an image to grab attention, provoke curiosity and pull us further into interaction with God.

LEADER'S NOTE

The following four points are included in slide 40.

Click once for each point.

Exercise Instructions 40

- Read the two passages on pages 65-66 again.
- What images do you see in your mind's eye?
- Try to capture what you see in some art form. (Have the participants use the space provided in their guide.)
- Remember: respond to each other with a "yes" attitude.

Debriefing and Conclusion
If we were going to do an entire Scripture study right now, we would keep all of our work in plain view as we pursued a closer study of the words of the passage. Some groups may even want to go back and redo the project, creating a new image with the new information they've learned through the course of the study. A "Yes" session can be as creative and imaginative as you want it to be: drawing, painting, sculpting, acting, writing poetry, making collages and so on. And many people discover that even in private Scripture study, opening up the imagination and coming at the Word of God from an image-based direction enhances their experience.

G. WORSHIP IN THE EMERGING CULTURE (15-20 MINUTES)* 41

"The style of worship songs that Martin Luther introduced was radical for his day. Luther made use of melodies from popular folk songs, which were seen as irreverent by established church authorities. Generations later they are considered a traditional, standardized form of conservative evangelical worship. . . . Luther's worship was a product of cultural and religious factors." Andy Park, *To Know You More,* p. 242

Sally Morganthaler Interview 42

Sally Morganthaler is one of the leading experts on worship in the emerging culture. She has written a couple of books on the topic, including *Worship Evangelism,* and is a consultant for many churches in the area of worship. (At the end of the video, ask participants for their responses to the interview.)

WORSHIP PRINCIPLES IN THE EMERGING CULTURE*

43

LEADER'S NOTE

This section shows the changes in worship from the modern to the emerging culture. The following points are included in slide 43.

Click once for each point.

MODERN	EMERGING
Individual	*Community*

In the past (and for many people today), worship centered around the individual and his or her relationship with God. However, as we have been reminded in the emerging culture, God created us to live in community not isolated from each other. Therefore, worship needs to draw us together in community.

Self-focused	*God Focused*

In the emerging culture we have moved from centering everything on the self to making the community central. However, Christians need to realize that not only were we created to be in community with each other, but even more importantly we were created to be in community with God. Therefore, our worship should not be centered around the individual or community but focused on God.

Spectator	*Participant*

Too often in recent modern culture most of us were mere spectators in worship. The worship service was centered around the choir and organ or piano in more traditional services, or around the song leader or band in contemporary services. People today do not want to observe but to actively participate in worship.

Programmatic	*Extemporaneous*

In worship services in most churches, all the components have been carefully programmed, leaving little to the imagination or spontaneity. While careful planning is helpful, we need to allow for God to work in more unrehearsed ways.

Excellence	*Authentic*

Not only have many worship services been programmed too tightly, the emphasis has been too much on excellence. While excellence has merit, it can sometimes come across as too perfect, lacking in authenticity. In today's culture people desire to see real people who express genuine joy in worship. Authenticity is valued over excellence.

One Style *Multiple Styles*

In recent years churches have engaged in major "worship wars" over what style of worship is right for their congregation. Should we have the traditional organ worship services of the middle 1900s, the contemporary guitar or piano services of the 1970s, or the more progressive band services of the 1990s? What we need to see in the twenty-first century is multiple styles of worship that are appropriate for the theme of a given worship service.

Christian or Seeker *Christian and Seeker*

During the last twenty years, churches have wrestled over who is the target audience of the church service. If the target audience is the "seeker," then the worship tends to be more generic so it won't offend the seeker. What we are finding out in today's emerging culture is that the seeker wants to experience a "Christian" worship service, not a toned-down service. It is critical for them to belong to a community and to experience God before they will believe in God.

Worship Discussion Questions*

- Why does a discussion on worship evoke such emotion among Christians?

- Why does our practice of worship need to change in the emerging culture?

- What changes does our church or ministry need to make?

- How do we set up a process for change in our worhsip that will unify and not divide our church?

H. PREACHING IN THE EMERGING CULTURE (15-20 MINUTES)* 45

"Instead of an exercise in transferring information so that people have a coherent well-informed worldview or belief system, preaching in the emerging culture aims at inspiring transformation. . . . Preaching becomes less and less a well-reasoned argument and more and more a shared practice among preacher and hearers. The preacher becomes less scholar and more sage. Less lecturer and more prophet." Brian McLaren, *Leadership Journal*, summer 2003, p. 36

Brian McLaren Interview 46

Brian McLaren is pastor of an emerging culture church in metro D.C. He is continuing to learn what it means to preach in this emerging culture. (At the end of the video, ask the participants for their responses.)

What are some of the emerging preaching characteristics? Here is a beginning list.

LEADER'S NOTE

Each of the seven points are included in slide 47.

Click once to advance to the next point.

NARRATIVE PREACHING: EMERGING CHARACTERISTICS* 47

- ***Part of a larger worship experience.*** Instead of being the primary attraction in our worship services today, preaching, though very important, should be a part of the larger worship experience.
- ***Multiple preaching voices.*** To recognize that God's Word, and not the preacher, is authoritative, and to recognize that God has given many people the gift of preaching and teaching, we need multiple preaching voices in our congregation.
- ***Development of trust with audience.*** Since positional authority is less important in the emerging culture, to be effective the preacher needs to develop trust with the audience over time. Preachers need to share stories from their own life journey so the congregation can identify with the messenger and the message.
- ***Conversational style.*** So people can identify with the speaker and be willing to respond to the message, the speaker needs to emphasize a more conversational than oratory style of preaching.
- ***Use of word and image.*** As we move more and more to an image-based culture, we need to recognize that God has communicated through images since the beginning of time. As communicators of God's Word, we need to make sure we also make use of image, not only to meet people where they are at but to communicate God's story.
- ***Connect the audience's story with God's kingdom story.*** People today need to see that God is relevant to their own life situation *and* that their life is part of a much bigger picture. They need a vision of God's kingdom story.
- ***Mission focused.*** A large part of God's kingdom story is God's mission. In our preaching we need to make sure we not only immerse ourselves in either our individual or our church's life, we need to focus on God's mission and God's role for us in accomplishing his mission.

USING IMAGINATION IN PREACHING AND TEACHING 48

In light of what we have learned about word and image in communication, you might be feeling like every Sunday sermon now has to be as visually innovative and exciting as the burning bush! Most of us who are preachers and teachers are neither artists nor designers of full multimedia experiences. Most of us have been trained to present word-based sermons.

Hopefully, the emerging culture will open up avenues for people gifted in the arts to use their talents in communicating the gospel. However, that doesn't mean the rest of us should simply give up preaching the gospel! This section will give the communicator some helpful tips on how to use the power of images and words in a typical presentation.

There is a great deal of variety among different church traditions in how images are (or are not) used. Some of the following suggestions may be standard practice in your church traditions; others may not suit your church at all. This list is not exhaustive, but it may help awaken your communication imagination.

Ethos, Logos, Pathos

LEADER'S NOTE

These three points are covered within slide 48.

Click once for each of the points.

In Aristotle's *Rhetoric,* which remains one of the premier works on public speaking even today, he describes three forms of appeal—ethos, logos and pathos:

1. *Ethos* is the establishment of credibility with the audience; it has to do with why the audience should listen. The word *ethic* comes from the Greek *ethos.* A public speaker builds ethos with deeds done. Ethos relates to credentials, relevant experience or connections made between the speaker and the audience.

2. *Logos* is the presentation of an argument. You build logos through a logical, reasonable case. Logos is the claim to the truth of the presentation.

3. *Pathos* appeals to the emotions of the audience. It's the emotional claim that causes the audience to care about the issue at hand. Pathos is connected to the passion of a speaker.

Often, today's sermons follow an outline of ethos followed by logos. Ethos is most recognizable with guest preachers. Guest preachers will almost always begin with a story about the local pastor, about the church itself or with some form of connection to the hometown. Sometimes, speakers will also mention reasons why they are qualified to speak on the day's topic. Once a speaker has established trust with the audience, he or she moves into the body of the sermon, the logos. In many church traditions, pathos is often left out completely. Yet in others the sermon ends with pathos, an emotional appeal to the audience to make some kind of commitment (e.g., an altar call).

Put Pathos in Its Place

The burning bush episode suggests a different approach: pathos, then ethos, followed by logos. The burning bush was essentially the use of an image to evoke pathos: it was an appeal to the emotions. Placing the pathos at the beginning of a sermon prepares the congregation emotionally to receive the message. Often, the listeners need pathos early in the sermon to jar them out of complacency so they can receive the logos.

The appeal to pathos can be accomplished through the use of an image, such as a film clip or a dramatic presentation or even a story that awakens the imagination. Awakening the imagination is usually the most effective way to pathos. However, even if you choose not to use images at all, you can still gain something from using a new outline for organizing your sermon.

Communicating to the Whole Person

In your preparation for a sermon or talk, ask yourself

- What emotions are people likely to feel about this topic?
- What passions will be awakened?
- Why should people care?
- How can I help people access these emotions?

For true transformation to occur, people need their whole being to be under the influence of the gospel message, not just their minds (or emotions, for that matter). The combination of pathos and logos helps people to do so.

USING VIDEO CLIPS WELL 49

In some church traditions, using a video clip in a sermon is a way to add an image to the teaching. It's not the *only* way (we'll discuss others later), but it's also not a bad idea. Movies are readily accessible, and referring to a movie is an easy way for someone not skilled in creating images to tap into the lives of others. Of course, simply plugging a video clip into a sermon does not mean that the biblical imagination is automatically enlivened.

Here are a few tips for effective use of video clips in your preaching or teaching:

LEADER'S NOTE

The following six points are covered within slide 49.

Click once for each.

- Make sure the clip is *appropriate for your audience.* Sometimes it is very tempting to stretch the boundaries of suitability, either to show how cutting-edge you are or because the clip seems to be perfect for your purposes. But a clip with questionable content will detract from rather than enhance the message. You don't want the big Sunday brunch discussion to be "What did you think of the pastor showing *that* clip?"
- Using a video clip is to a certain extent a public endorsement of the film, so make sure it's *a movie you wouldn't mind recommending.* Be aware that if the clip you show is com-

pelling, people will want to watch the entire movie. If the clip itself is appropriate but you wouldn't recommend the entire movie, you may not want to use the clip.

- Make sure you *have the right technology.* You don't need to be completely state-of-the-art, but if your technology is clunky to the point of distraction, the clip won't do its job. Despite what you lose in the power to attract the eye, you may want to describe the scene rather than show the clip. Tell the story as vibrantly as you can, and it will probably be more useful than a clip people can't see or hear well.
- *Shorter is better.* Commercials communicate in under one minute. For our purposes, more than ten minutes is too long and less than five is probably best. Clips should be long enough for the audience to make sense of what is going on, but you don't need to tell the complete story. In fact, it's best to leave people wanting more. Remember, an image is used to attract attention to what you are going to say next.
- *Don't explain.* If you need to spend a long time prefacing or interpreting your clip, it's not the right one to use. People should be able to see what you want them to see in the clip just by watching it. If you need to explain the clip, you are helping people understand the film, but the film is not helping people understand your message.
- *Don't expect the film to preach.* Often we look for a video clip that will say exactly what we want to say, but *you* should make the main points yourself. Clips are best for provoking questions, sparking identification or creating the right emotional environment, not giving answers.

[JESUS IMAGE WITH CROSS BANNER] 50

You don't need to be a great artist to create powerful images. Even very simple visual aids can be quite effective in enhancing a message. Just a little attention to what people are seeing can make a great deal of difference. Of course, some church traditions already do an excellent job of paying attention to the visual experience. In liturgical traditions some of the visual aids are quite elaborate: altarpieces and stained-glass windows portray important stories from the Scripture or remind people of the glory of God. Ask the participants what they think this image of Jesus (slide 50) portrays. However, some of the visual choices are powerfully subtle.

SIMPLE VISUAL EFFECTS 51

LEADER'S NOTE

The points are covered within slide 51.

Click once for each.

- A raised lectern shows respect for the Word of God.

- The lifting of the communion cup focuses attention on Jesus' shed blood.
- The breaking of the bread reminds us of Jesus' broken body.
- A simple black cloth draped over the cross during Lent communicates mourning.

Even nonliturgical churches unconsciously make choices about the visual effect on the congregation. As we've discussed earlier, people's eyes are naturally restless. They search for the most interesting item to focus on, whether that's the preacher's tie, the large white word "Yamaha" on the electric keyboard or the slight movements of the people.

- Just a little thought and attention can create visual effects that focus people's attention and add to the message rather than leaving their eyes to wander.
- Projecting a relevant painting onto a screen will subtly enhance people's appreciation of the message.
- Use meaningful, symbolic gestures when speaking. One way to do this is to act out a single gesture from the passage (for example, the embrace the father gives to the prodigal son, Jesus reaching down to save Peter from falling into the sea, Aaron and Hur holding up Moses' hands). Repeatedly use this gesture to emphasize a point in your sermon. It becomes a small picture of what you are trying to describe, a symbol that can easily be referred to.
- Dress the stage with a lit candle, a banquet table or some other item pertinent to the message.
- Give people something sacred to see. Although visual statements relevant to the day's topic are most helpful, even a simple cross in plain view can remind people of the holiness of the moment and enhance their experience.

QUESTIONS ON PREACHING IN THE EMERGING CULTURE*

LEADER'S NOTE

The following questions are covered with slide 52.

Click once for each.

- What posture should a preacher take in relationship to the audience?
- In an image-based culture, why might a few good stories be more important than a three-point outline?
- How can stories carry the point of the sermon?

- Why is it important to use the imagination in sermons today?
- How can we help people today see the power of God's Word for transforming our lives?

I. COMMUNICATION QUESTIONS (5-10 MINUTES)* 53

LEADER'S NOTE

The following points are covered within slide 53.

Click once for each.

---

1. What are the different roles words and images have in communication in the emerging culture?

2. How might our Bible study, worship and preaching need to change in light of God's work in this emerging culture?

Select Resources

The Church on the Other Side by Brian McLaren
The Emerging Church by Dan Kimball
The Great Worship Awakening by Robb Redman
Preaching in a Postmodern World by Graham Johnston
To Know You More by Andy Park
Transforming Bible Study by Robert Grahmann
Worship Evangelism by Sally Morganthaler

5
Context

OVERVIEW

INTRODUCTION*

This module addresses a worldview shift from macronarrative (a large, all-encompassing story) to micronarratives (small, tribal stories). The changes in our culture during the last fifty years in this area are profound. The focus of the module is multiethnicity and the call to the church to embody the gospel that reaches across ethnic and cultural boundaries.

QUESTIONS COVERED*

- How have the world and North America changed over the last forty years?
- How have these changes affected or should have affected our ministries?
- According to the Scriptures, how does God want the church to minister in a multiethnic society?
- What changes need to happen in my church or ministry as a result of these societal changes?

CONTENT FLOW

Here is a suggested arrangement of the learning components in this module. Use the components to customize the training for your audience and time frame.

A. Introduction: Changing Face of the World (5-10 minutes)

B. Changing Face of the United States (15-20 minutes)

C. Context Transitions (5-10 minutes)

D. Scripture Study (30-40 minutes)

E. The Civil Rights Movement: A Case Study in Worldview Transition (10-30 minutes)

F. Scripture Study (30-40 minutes)

G. Alex Gee and Steve Hayner Interview (10-15 minutes)

H. Where Do We Go from Here? (10-20 minutes)

WORLDVIEW: FROM TRIBALISM TO GOD'S KINGDOM STORY 1

A. INTRODUCTION: CHANGING FACE OF THE WORLD
(5-10 MINUTES)

CHANGING FACE OF THE WORLD 2

The changes that have taken place within North America and in the world in the last four decades are extraordinary. Nations that threatened Western society with destruction in the past aren't even mentioned on the nightly news, while others that we hadn't even heard of in 1960 are on everyone's lips. Daily we use technology that is far beyond the imagination of the science fiction of forty years ago. How we entertain ourselves, where we live, our relationships, how we raise our children—it's all completely different now. Even what we eat today would have been considered exotic in 1960. Think about it, does anyone in America consider a taco or gyro "foreign food" anymore?

LEADER'S NOTE

Each of the following points is included within slide 2.

Click once to advance to each point.

Globalization

In one sense the people of the world have never been as close as they are today. People can instantaneously communicate with someone on the other side of the world through e-mail or cell phones. What formerly took weeks to accomplish now takes seconds. Economically the world is closely connected. A political, economic or natural disaster in one part of the world can automatically affect the price of oil or groceries on the other side of the world. For better or worse television has given the world a certain image of the West, especially the United States.

Tribalization

Even though the world has never been closer, it is moving further apart culturally and ethnically. People used to think that when communism was defeated, the whole world would become united and democratic. However, just the opposite may take place. Instead of economic differences, we are now faced with more fundamental problems, such as ethnic and religious differences. The world is becoming more tribalized.

Immigration

Tribalization is occurring in the midst of one of the greatest migrations in history. Worldwide, people from the Middle East are migrating to Europe; South and Central Americans are migrating to the United States; and many Asian people are migrating to Canada and the United States. Many countries are experiencing a large influx of people who are very different from their traditional ethnic groups. The world's ethnic distribution is rapidly changing.

All these changes should be influencing the way churches are doing ministry in the coming years. Let's look at one country, the United States, to see how immigration is changing it.

B. CHANGING FACE OF THE UNITED STATES (15-20 MINUTES)

LEADER'S NOTE

John Long oversees the census analysis team for the United States Census Bureau. His interview is designed to help us see how and why U.S. demographics have been changing over the last forty years and what changes are projected in the next forty years.

JOHN LONG INTERVIEW 

United States Census*

1960		**2000**		**2040 (projected)**	
White	88%	White	69%	White	54%
Black	10%	Black	13%	Black	14%
Latino	<1%	Latino	13%	Latino	22%
Asian	<1%	Asian	4%	Asian	7%
Multiracial	——	Multiracial	2%	Multiracial	2%

Perhaps the greatest change is in the ethnic makeup of the U.S. population. The respective 1960 and 2000 census reports and the 2040 projections reveal some fascinating and telling differences.

DISCUSSION: CHANGING FACE OF YOUR COMMUNITY* 

- What did you learn about how and why the United States is changing demographically?

- What are the demographics for your community?

- How have the demographics of your community changed in the last fifteen years?

- How has your church or ministry changed its mission in light of these changes?

- Why is it important that we respond?

C. CONTEXT TRANSITIONS (5-10 MINUTES)* 6

LEADER'S NOTE

Each of the following points is included within slide 6.

Click once to advance to each point.

MODERN	POSTMODERN	CHRISTIAN
World Unity	*Tribalism*	*God's Kingdom*

Up to at least the middle of the twentieth century, much of the world expected international unity and cooperation under the auspices of such organizations as the League of Nations or the United Nations. But as the century ended, instead of becoming more unified the world has become more tribalized, with little hope or desire for unity. Into this mix the church needs to demonstrate the unity of the kingdom of God, giving people a picture of the type of community God desires for all humans.

Human Progress — *Human Cynicism* — *Eternal Hope*

It was proclaimed in 1900 that the twentieth century would be "mankind's" greatest century. The expectation of human progress and the desire for the domination of nature turned to cynicism by the end of the century. Christians in the twenty-first century need to demonstrate hope not in humankind but in God.

Individualism — *Tolerance* — *Agape Love*

In the past century we moved from a heightened view of the rights of the individual to a begrudging tolerance of people different from us. The church must take a firm stand and in word and deed proclaim that God's agape love demonstrates a much higher view of humankind than a mere tolerance of others.

Integration — *Ethnicity* — *Multiethnicity*

From the beginning to the second half of the twentieth century, there was a concerted effort to integrate all ethnic groups into a melting pot. However, those who valued their ethnicity eventually realized that their heritage and traditions were being diminished. Thus they rejected the melting pot and began to emphasize their ethnicity. The church needs to show the world that we can have unity within our multiethnicity (without diminishing our own ethnicity).

A MISSIONAL CALL TO THE CHURCH* 7

"Our generation, without necessarily knowing it, is calling the church back to what the church has always been called to be—a multi-generational, multi-cultural, open, orthodox and culturally engaged body of believers. This is what the church will need to be in order to speak to the postmodern culture with any legitimacy." (Dieter Zander, *Re:Generation Quarterly* 5, no. 3, p. 19)

D. SCRIPTURE STUDY (30-40 MINUTES)*

This Scripture examines a key transition in Scripture. The issues in the text form the backdrop for our experiences of ethnicity today. The study affirms God's involvement in cultural transition.

Genesis 11:1-10

Now the whole earth had one language and the same words. [2]And as they migrated from the east, they came upon a plain in the land of Shinar and settled there. [3]And they said to one another, "Come, let us make bricks, and burn them thoroughly." And they had brick for stone, and bitumen for mortar. [4]Then they said, "Come, let us build ourselves a city, and a tower with its top in the heavens, and let us make a name for ourselves; otherwise we shall be scattered abroad upon the face of the whole earth." [5]The LORD came down to see the city and the tower, which mortals had built. [6]And the LORD said, "Look, they are one people, and they have all one language; and this is only the beginning of what they will do; nothing that they propose to do will now be impossible for them. [7]Come, let us go down, and confuse their language there, so that they will not understand one another's speech." [8]So the LORD scattered them abroad from there over the face of all the earth, and they left off building the city. [9]Therefore it was called Babel, because there the LORD confused the language of all the earth; and from there the LORD scattered them abroad over the face of all the earth.

[10]These are the descendants of Shem. When Shem was one hundred years old, he became the father of . . .

Genesis 12:1-3

Now the LORD said to Abram, "Go from your country and your kindred and your father's house to the land that I will show you. [2]I will make of you a great nation, and I will bless you, and make your name great, so that you will be a blessing. [3]I will bless those who bless you, and the one who curses you I will curse; and in you all the families of the earth shall be blessed."

Commentary

Genesis 11 ends the opening section of Genesis, which describes the increasing alienation between humans and between God and humans. Genesis 12 begins the story of God's saving activity.

The word *nation* often designates an ethnic group in the Old Testament.

Notice what happens with "name." The nations try to make a name for themselves. God is making a name for Abraham.

Regardless of your understanding of why God acts, God clearly takes responsibility for ethnic diversity and the confusion of language. Throughout Scripture God acts for the good of his creation!

OBSERVATION QUESTIONS* 9

1. What did the people of Babel desire?

2. What resources did they have to achieve their desires?

3. What did these people fear?

4. What was wrong with their desires?

5. What was God's kingdom story? (Refer to Genesis 1:28.)

INTERPRETATION QUESTIONS* 10

1. How were the people of Babel thwarting God's kingdom story?

2. What are the differences between how these people and Abram (and his family) responded to God's kingdom story?

3. How was God using Abram to accomplish God's kingdom story?

APPLICATION QUESTIONS* 11 

1. What have you learned about God's kingdom story?

2. In what ways are your desires (and your ministry's desires) similar or different to God's desires?

3. How does God want to bless "all peoples" through your church or ministry?

4. What specific ways does God want your church or ministry to reach out to other ethnic groups in your surrounding community?

E. THE CIVIL RIGHTS MOVEMENT: A CASE STUDY IN WORLDVIEW TRANSITION (10-30 MINUTES)

TONY WARNER INTERVIEW 12

LEADER'S NOTE

Tony Warner is InterVarsity's Associate Regional Director in the Southeast. He is a long-time cultural observer and has become an expert in the history of the Civil Rights Movement.

THE CIVIL RIGHTS MOVEMENT: A CASE STUDY IN TRANSITIONAL CONTEXT

LEADER'S NOTE

"Modern culture" is defined here as a Eurocentric, Enlightenment-influenced culture.

Modern Culture

- Confidence in human reason
- Belief in societal progress
- Humanity's problems should be solved by reason
- Spirit of optimism: There was a hope that humankind was heading toward a kind of universal knowledge: all people would eventually come to the same conclusions; if we just thought long and hard enough, our collective intellect would lead us to truth. There would be a grand metanarrative, a universal defining story, that would be shaped by reason and science and would lead society to a new level of harmony and understanding.

Some Definitions

There are key distinctions between *culture, ethnicity* and *race.*

Culture

Culture is what we make of our environment and the world around us. It is how we become socialized in the world. Culture is dynamic and changing. Culture is how we see ourselves and other people who are different from us. All culture has good, bad and neutral elements.

Ethnicity

Ethnicity is the specific people group we were born into. Ethnicity is God-given and does not change. There is cultural diversity within every ethnic group.

Race

Race is a made-up concept, a social construction that became highly developed during the Enlightenment (roughly A.D. 1500-1800). It developed further through the economic advantages of the slave trade. Physiological and natural science during this time were based on the idea that race determined a wide range of human traits (intelligence, temperament, etc.). The advent of the study of genetics has scientifically disproven these beliefs.

LEADER'S NOTE

Each of the following main points is included within slides 13-14.

Click once to advance to each point.

HISTORICAL OVERVIEW* 13-14

The First and Second World Wars Shake Optimism

The sheer folly and waste of human life in World War I led many optimists to believe that the world would learn its lesson and not repeat such horrors, hence the dubbing of WWI the "war to end all wars." When it was followed less than twenty years later by the rise of fascism, WWII, holocausts in Europe and Asia, and wholesale atomic destruction, few were able to maintain their optimism. The idea of human progress seemed less and less tenable. While modern optimism did not immediately disappear (particularly in America—witness the unbridled faith in science during the 1950s), it went into serious decline after 1945.

European Colonialism Unravels

In the 1930s and 1940s, Gandhi and Nehru led a nonviolent movement against the British, resulting in independence for India (and the creation of Pakistan) in 1947. After liberating it from the Japanese, the United States granted independence to the Philippines in 1946, and Indonesia received independence from the Dutch in 1949. During the 1950s and 1960s, virtually all of Africa received its independence from colonial powers, as did much of the Caribbean and Pacific Islands.

Non-European Nationalism Ascends

Gandhi's example led to widespread nationalism among the educated classes in nations other than India and left a lasting impression on many black Americans, most importantly a young preacher named Martin Luther King Jr. In the wake of the Civil Rights movement, many other immigrant and ethnic groups began to have a heightened sense of identity. In 1965, immigration laws were radically changed; quotas that intentionally limited the number of nonwhite immigrants were abolished. Different ethnic groups shared common struggles and pain: the internment of Japanese-American citizens during World War II is a good example.

Global Evil Shakes Idea of Societal Progress

America's "metanarrative" has been very important to our sense of optimism and purpose, and has been instrumental in its success, ideology and theology. This metanarrative is fueled by the American's belief that the United States is inherently good: it is a "city set on a hill," a light and inspiration to the nations, blessed by God, the hope of humanity and the protector of individual rights and freedom. This vision sustained U.S. citizens through the Cold War. It is important to remember that this optimistic vision of America transcended political ideology: conservatives and liberals, Democrats and Republicans held it in common. Today, there is great concern over the steady erosion of this vision. In addition to events mentioned above, the vision was weakened further during the 1960s and 1970s by racial violence, the national trauma of Vietnam and the horrors of the Khmer Rouge in Cambodia. In addition, the holocausts in Rwanda and Bosnia, the strife in Israel and the brutality of America's inner cities make it seem foolish and naive to be optimistic. Despite a temporary return to American idealism in the wake of 9/11, it seems unlikely that this is more than veneer.

KEY FEATURES OF THE CIVIL RIGHTS MOVEMENT*

The Beloved Community

The beloved community was the motivating vision of the leaders of the Civil Rights Movement. It was the concept of the kingdom of God on earth. Though there were different theological perspectives within the movement, this vision of God's kingdom spurred the fight against racism and segregation in the South. It was no accident that the theme of the Birmingham campaign was "Redeeming the Soul of America."

The Principle of Nonviolence

Dr. King and others identified two possible responses to the evils of segregation. The first, a passive response, accepted evil as an inevitable fact of the human condition; this response was adopted as a matter of survival for black people in the South. The second, violence, was either self-destructive and suicidal or a futile, angry gesture of defiance toward the white power structure. The Civil Rights Movement crafted a way for black people to respond effectively to the injustice around them in a nonviolent way.

King's philosophy (1) is nonviolent resistance, not passive nonresistance, (2) seeks friendship with, not humiliation of, the adversary, (3) is directed against the "forces of evil," not the person committing the evil, (4) is willing to accept suffering in order to achieve a goal, (5) avoids internal "violence of the spirit" as much as it avoids physical violence and refuses to hate an opponent, and (6) believes that God is on the side of justice no matter how things appear at the moment.

Movement from Optimism to Pessimism

Many naturally optimistic Americans, black and white, saw this movement as an opportunity to quickly correct the problems of segregation, injustice and racism. They believed that once people became aware of the problem and understood the evil, they would be quick to rectify it. However, many in the movement underestimated the biblical truth of the fallenness of humanity. Though there were great successes, there were also many setbacks and tragedies. Many moved from a naive optimism to a very bitter pessimism.

1964—A Critical Year

Assassination and Protest

1963 ended with the assassination of President Kennedy and the bombing of a black church in Birmingham, Alabama, that killed four little girls. (Note: In 2002, the three surviving bombers were tried, convicted and sentenced to life in prison, nearly forty years after the crime—whether this is seen as reason for optimism or pessimism is no doubt dependent on the individual's disposition.) During 1964 there were major civil rights campaigns in Alabama and Florida as well as a major summer program of SNCC (Student Non-violent Coordinating Committee) in which 1,000 young people, mostly college students from the North, descended on Mississippi to challenge the system of segregation.

Civil Rights Bill

The U.S. Civil Rights Bill was passed in 1964. It was the year that the FBI began trying to discredit Dr. King via extensive electronic surveillance of his public and private life. During the 1964 Democratic National Convention in Atlantic City, amid riveting vocal challenges to the all-white Mississippi delegation by people like Fannie Lou Hamer, President Lyndon Johnson personally prevented the delegation from being heard over the airwaves. The sense of betrayal caused by this act opened the floodgates of despair and cynicism. The system could not be trusted, even when controlled by supposedly "friendly" forces.

War

The War on Poverty began in 1964, the same year as the Gulf of Tonkin resolution (which gave President Johnson a free hand in Vietnam, where he rapidly built up American troops), and the Beatles invasion (which introduced black musical styles into mainstream American culture far beyond anything previous). Politically, 1964 was the last time the majority of blacks and whites voted along the same lines. Malcolm X broke away from the Nation of Islam, and his message of black pride took fire in the black community.

Changes in the Civil Rights Movement*

Loss of Confidence in Modernist Attempts to Correct Past Racial Injustice

We have already referred to racial injustice above, specifically in regard to President Johnson's betrayal of African Americans at the Democratic National Convention, along with the general persistence of racial strife in the South and elsewhere in America.

Shift from Metanarrative to Micronarratives

As entrenched attitudes proved resistant to change, the American metanarrative gave way to a plethora of micronarratives—black, white, Asian, Latino, male, female, gay, straight and so forth.

Loss of Confidence in the Free Enterprise System

Those traditionally denied the wealth and benefits of the free market system challenged the Cold War tendency to look at the world through the simplistic lens of communism and capitalism. While both systems were problematic for the non-European world, the strongest proponents of capitalism were the very people who were least interested in the agendas of nonwhite peoples.

Challenges to the Dominant European Perspective

As non-European voices were heard, many old assumptions were revealed as the "dominant view" masquerading as truth. "Truth" is determined by those with the power.

LASTING IMPLICATIONS*

15

The fall of humanity into sin has had many lasting effects, not least of which are racial strife and dysfunction. The redeeming work of Christ and the Holy Spirit transforms our bad multiethnic relationships, making us a people who reflect more the character of God.

Among Whites

Paternalism. A deep awareness of past injustice has often led whites to feel sorry for black people. But while their hearts are broken, their guilt has not been released to God. This leads to paternalism toward black people, with a continuing grip on power over their community.

Hostility. Because they fear revenge by blacks for past injustices (again, there is an underlying feeling of guilt), many whites take measures to make sure it doesn't happen. Hostility toward blacks is manifested particularly among extremist and "white power" groups. They expect black people to be violent and untrustworthy.

Ignoring the problem. Some white people try to avoid guilt altogether. They take a "historical" approach but don't like to be reminded of real history. They tend to say things like, "I didn't own any slaves; my family came as immigrants" and "Blacks have great advantages now; in fact they're better off than whites in many ways." They have a real antipathy to so-called political correctness.

Among Blacks

Anger. Angry blacks have a tendency to blame racism and "the white man" for everything. When this anger is not dealt with, it becomes all-consuming; it becomes a god. White people in this country have responsibility and advantages, but they are not all-powerful.

Self-hatred. When anger turns in on itself, it becomes self-hatred. Some black people have tremendous self-loathing and despise much of their own heritage. Everything about their own people is seen in negative terms, and they develop a tendency to imitate whites.

Despair. Sometimes there is a pervasive hopelessness in the black community. Change in society or among whites is deemed impossible, therefore contact with whites is minimized.

Among Both Whites and Blacks

The "American Dream" mentality. "I worked hard for what I have. Everyone else can do the same." There is hostility toward those who do not "pull themselves up by their own bootstraps." A high value is placed on assimilation. This is often an "immigrant mentality."

High value placed on rules. A feeling has developed among some people that no one should get any breaks. Society's rules are good and must be observed by all. These people are opposed to affirmative action. Nonwhites may just need to overcompensate to prove their worthiness.

Political correctness. Liberals often think that racial problems can be solved through rules and "correct" language. This is basically a surface technique ill-equipped to deal with the deeper problems of sinful hearts.

Discussion Questions

- How have the Civil Rights Movement of the 1950s and 1960s and the changes in the immigration laws of the 1960s affected the United States?

- How has the church responded to these changing dynamics?

- How has your church or ministry responded to these ethnic changes?

- What attitude and lifestyle should the church adopt today to minister in this ethnically diverse emerging culture?

F. SCRIPTURE STUDY (30-40 MINUTES)*

Acts 2:1-12

When the day of Pentecost had come, they were all together in one place. [2]And suddenly from heaven there came a sound like the rush of a violent wind, and it filled the entire house where they were sitting. [3]Divided tongues, as of fire, appeared among them, and a tongue rested on each of them. [4]All of them were filled with the Holy Spirit and began to speak in other languages, as the Spirit gave them ability.

[5]Now there were devout Jews from every nation under heaven living in Jerusalem. [6]And at this sound the crowd gathered and was bewildered, because each one heard them speaking in the native language of each. [7]Amazed and astonished, they asked, "Are not all these who are speaking Galileans? [8]And how is it that we hear, each of us, in our own native language? [9]Parthians, Medes, Elamites, and residents of Mesopotamia, Judea and Cappadocia, Pontus and Asia, [10]Phrygia and Pamphylia, Egypt and the parts of Libya belonging to Cyrene, and visitors from Rome, both Jews and proselytes, [11]Cretans and Arabs—in our own languages we hear them speaking about God's deeds and power." [12]All

were amazed and perplexed, saying to one another, "What does this mean?"

REVELATION 21:1-7

Then I saw a new heaven and a new earth; for the first heaven and the first earth had
passed away, and the sea was no more. [2]And I saw the holy city, the new Jerusalem, coming down out of heaven from God, prepared as a bride adorned for her husband. [3]And I
heard a loud voice from the throne saying,

"See the home of God is among mortals.
He will dwell with them as their God;
they will be his peoples,
and God himself will be with them;
[4]he will wipe every tear from their eyes.
Death will be no more;
mourning and crying and pain will be no more,
for the first things have passed away."

[5]And the one who was seated on the throne said, "See, I am making all things new."
Also he said, "Write this, for these words are trustworthy and true." [6]Then he said to me,
"It is done! I am the Alpha and the Omega, the beginning and the end. To the thirsty I
will give water as a gift from the spring of the water of life. [7]Those who conquer will in-
herit these things, and I will be their God and they will be my children."

OBSERVATION QUESTIONS* 18

1. What happens at Pentecost?

2. What happens in the New Jerusalem?

3. What does God do at Pentecost?

4. What does God do in the New Jerusalem?

INTERPRETATION QUESTIONS* 19

1. How are the events at Pentecost a reversal of the events at the Tower of Babel?

2. What is the significance that all these nations were represented at Pentecost?

3. How are the events in the New Jerusalem a fulfillment of God's original plan?

4. Why should all of these events give us hope for the future?

Application Questions*

1. How would you describe God's kingdom story? 20

2. What is the significance for your church or ministry that God is the God of all ethnicities and that he desires to bring these ethnicities together?

3. What does that mean for your own ethnic identity?

4. What does that mean for your church's ethnic identities?

G. Alex Gee and Steve Hayner Interview 21

(10-15 MINUTES)

Steve Hayner, former president of InterVarsity Christian Fellowship, and Alex Gee, pastor of Fountain of Life in Madison, Wisconsin, worked together in Alex's church and within InterVarsity. This video describes what they have learned from their partnership.

Interview Discussion 22

- How were Alex and Steve able to develop their friendship and partnership?

- Along the way, what did they learn about each other's cultures?

- Why is a friendship like Steve and Alex's and a multiethnic church like Fountain of Life such a powerful witness in this emerging culture?

- What opportunities do you, your church or your ministry have to develop multiethnic friendships and partnerships?

H. WHERE DO WE GO FROM HERE? (10-20 MINUTES)*

23

LEADER'S NOTE

Break into small groups and ask the groups to discuss practical ways they might act in each of the following areas. Have them consider both steps they might take as individuals and as a church or ministry.

God's Kingdom of Agape Love

The integrative point for these matters is the love of the triune God as expressed in Jesus Christ's incarnation, life, death, resurrection and exaltation. The love of Christ is the basis for community among the people of God. It is also the motivation behind the desire to see the kingdom of God established in the world among God's people. God's love extends to all races and ethnic groups, so God's people are called not only to love all individuals but also all races and nations. God's ultimate goal is not just racial reconciliation but for all races and nations to worship and glorify him.

Fighting Injustice Together

The love of God requires justice for all ethnic groups and nations. This drives us to fight against forces of evil that seek to destroy certain races. Each racial and ethnic group that experiences oppression wrestles along with God over the fight against evil and the historic reality of racism. Each racial and ethnic group is called to work out what faithfulness to God looks like within the context of its own history.

Creating Room in Our Hearts

God's love for all peoples demands that we create space in our hearts for the "other" whom we would normally define as an enemy or adversary. This is true for every racial and ethnic group.

A Movement Toward Community

True community involves living lives of repentance before each other. Individuals must learn to ask for—and receive—forgiveness. God's love for all peoples permeates Scripture and is central to God's story of redemption. At the end, each tribe and nation will worship the Lamb as a member of their particular tribe and nation!

CONTEXT QUESTIONS* 24

1. Why does God care about how different ethnic and cultural groups get along?

2. How has immigration affected your community's ethnic identity?

3. What headway has your church or ministry made in developing multiethnic partnerships?

4. What opportunities does your church or ministry have to become more multiethnic?

5. How will your church or ministry need to change in order to become more multiethnic?

6
Implications

OVERVIEW

INTRODUCTION*

This module is designed for you and others to consider specific implications that ministering in this emerging culture might have in your church or ministry.

QUESTIONS COVERED*

- How do you and others in your ministry deal with change?
- Why is it necessary to make significant changes in ministry?
- Within this emerging culture, what are some of the ministry implications we need to consider in the following areas?
  leadership
  community
  spiritual formation
  reconciliation
  witness
  worship
  preaching
  worldview

CONTENT FLOW

The following is a suggested arrangement of the components in this module. Use the components to customize the material for your audience and time frame.

A. Introduction (5-10 minutes)

B. Scripture Study (20-30 minutes)

C. Transitioning into an Emerging Ministry: An Overview (5-10 minutes)

D. Empowering Leadership (10-20 minutes)

E. Missional Community (10-20 minutes)

F. Experiencing God (10-20 minutes)

G. Reconciling Gospel (10-20 minutes)

H. Great Commandment Witness (10-20 minutes)

I. Imaginative Worship (10-20 minutes)

J. Narrative Preaching (10-20 minutes)

K. God's Kingdom Story (10-20 minutes)

L. Emerging Hope (5-10 minutes)

IMPLICATIONS: TRANSITIONING INTO AN EMERGING MINISTRY

A. INTRODUCTION (5-10 MINUTES)*

If we are going to have a successful ministry in the emerging culture, we will need to make some changes in how we do ministry. For some of us change comes very easily; for others it comes with much anguish. In order to partner together to help our church or ministry make the necessary changes, we need to understand how we and others around us deal with change. Next, we will study a passage of Scripture to see how God wants us to act in times of cultural change. We have identified eight key elements of ministry that might need to change as we continue to minister in the emerging culture. We will look at what the ministry implications in each of these areas are. We can begin or continue to make the necessary changes in ministry in order to do what God has called us to.

DEALING WITH CHANGE*

LEADER'S NOTE

Each of the following questions are included in slide 2.

Click once to advance to each question.

- In general, how do you respond to change?

- How do other people in your church or ministry respond to change?

- On a scale of 1-5 (1 being most needed) rate your sense of need to make significant ministry changes in light of this transition into emerging culture. Rate your church's other leaders' and members' sense of need for ministry changes.

- What causes the differences in perception? How can you resolve these differences?

B. SCRIPTURE STUDY (20-30 MINUTES)*

3

BACKGROUND TO STUDY

Jesus is being confronted by the religious leaders of his day. Why, they ask, isn't Jesus following some of the cherished Jewish traditions? This passage gives Jesus' response to these questions and charges. Here we learn how Jesus might want us to respond to some of our present traditions that may need to change as we minister within this emerging culture.

LUKE 5:33-39

33 Then they said to him, "John's disciples, like the disciples of the Pharisees, frequently
fast and pray, but your disciples eat and drink." 34 Jesus said to them, "You cannot make
wedding guests fast while the bridegroom is with them, can you? 35 The days will come
when the bridegroom will be taken away from them, and then they will fast in those
days." 36 He also told them a parable: "No one tears a piece from a new garment and sews
it on an old garment: otherwise the new will be torn, and the piece from the new will not
match the old. 37 And no one puts new wine into old wineskins; otherwise the new wine
will burst the skins and will be spilled, and the skins will be destroyed. 38 But new wine
must be put into fresh wineskins. 39 And no one after drinking old wine desires new wine,
but says, 'The old is good.'"

LEADER'S NOTE

Each of the following points and questions are included in slide 3.

Click once to advance to each question.

ENTERING THE TEXT QUESTION*

What cherished tradition in your ministry is "off-limits" to change; that is, people would be terribly upset if it were deleted or changed?

OBSERVATION QUESTIONS*

1. What had the religious leaders up in arms?

2. What three examples does Jesus give for why his disciples are breaking tradition?

3. What happens when new wine is placed in old wineskins?

Interpretation Questions*

1. Why were the Pharisees so upset?
2. Why did Jesus think it was not appropriate to follow the fasting tradition at that time?
3. Why didn't Jesus want to place his ministry in the old wineskin structures of Judaism?
4. What did Jesus mean by "No one after drinking old wine wants the new"?

Application Questions*

1. Why is it hard for people to leave the old wine or wineskins for the new?
2. Why is it crucial for some new wineskins to be developed in this emerging culture?
3. What will happen if we don't develop some new wineskins?
4. What are the new wineskins that need to be developed in your church or ministry?

C. TRANSITIONING INTO AN EMERGING MINISTRY: AN OVERVIEW (5-10 MINUTES)*

We have identified eight ministry areas that need to be carefully examined if we are going to be faithful and successful in ministry in the emerging culture. We have already looked at these areas in the previous modules. Here they are arranged in an acrostic—EMERGING. We have probably made some headway in these areas, but none of us have "arrived."

LEADER'S NOTE

Each of the following points are included in slide 6.

Click once to advance to each point.

E*mpowering Leadership*
Leadership needs to be more about empowering and less about controlling.

M*issional Community*
The ethos of the church needs to be centered in a welcoming, inclusive and intimate community.

E*xperiencing God*
The community needs to experience God and not just know about God. This is the foundation for our spiritual formation.

R*econciling Gospel*
The gospel includes a journey in which we are reconciled to God, to each other and across ethnic and cultural distinctions

G*reat Commandment Witness*
Our most effective witness will be more about how we live than what we say. We need to show God's love and provide a place for people to belong.

I*maginative Worship*
Our focus in worship needs to be on God, not on us. It also needs to include all of our senses.

N*arrative Preaching*
The focus of preaching is to place our story (lives) in the context of God's overall story, from creation to completion.

G*od's Kingdom Story*
While recognizing that God's kingdom will not be fully established until Christ comes again, we need to be involved in establishing that kingdom today in our own lives, in our church and in local and international communities.

Each of these areas will be discussed in further detail. They are introduced by a quotation or video and followed up by a Bible study. Then we will discuss the ministry area's characteristics and end with important questions about it.

D. EMPOWERING LEADERSHIP (10-20 MINUTES)

KEN FONG INTERVIEW 7

LEADER'S NOTE

Ken Fong is pastor of Evergreen Baptist Church in the greater Los Angeles community.

EMPOWERING LEADERSHIP: BIBLICAL TEXT

Background

The purpose of the book of Ephesians is to envision what a Christian church looks like. In the church everyone has a role and gifts to be used in performing that role. The gifts and leadership roles are dispersed among many people, not just a few.

Ephesians 4:11-13 8

[11]The gifts he gave were that some would be apostles, some prophets, some evangelists,
some pastors and teachers, [12]to equip the saints for the work of ministry, for building up
the body of Christ, [13]until all of us come to the unity of the faith and of the knowledge
of the Son of God, to maturity, to the measure of the full stature of Christ.

Bible Study Questions

1. What does this passage tell us about who the gifts were given to?

2. What are the purposes of these gifts?

3. Are the gifts in your church or ministry centered on one or two leaders, or are they dispersed among many?

Empowering Leadership: Primary Characteristics*

Leadership Teams

Leadership is dispersed among many people who have different gifts. These people, instead of acting alone, need to be in teams to encourage, support and depend on each other. They form a community that emphasizes relationships and tasks.

Earned Authority

Leaders today need to recognize that authority doesn't automatically come with a position but needs to be earned through their actions *and* their character.

Empowering Others

The role of the team leader is not to control but to empower others to use their gifts for the betterment of the community and to accomplish the task.

Committed to Process

The process of accomplishing the goal is just as important as reaching the goal. People need to belong to a team that personally values them and their opinions.

Shared Vision

People need to be committed to a goal or vision that they believe in and have a part in shaping.

Inspiring Others to Lead

While in the past people aspired to leadership, people today need to be inspired to leadership. They do not feel worthy to lead, nor do they want to be set above the community.

QUESTIONS TO CONSIDER 10

- Is our present leadership structure more modern or emerging?

- What needs to change in our present leadership structure in order to more effectively minister in the emerging culture?*

- What are the stumbling blocks to change?

- What are the next steps we need to take?

E. MISSIONAL COMMUNITY (10-20 MINUTES)

BRIAN MCLAREN INTERVIEW

MISSIONAL COMMUNITY: BIBLICAL TEXT

BACKGROUND

This passage is set in the context of Jesus' prayer. He is praying that the disciples will continue the example that he set on earth of building a community in which all its members care for each other, which is a witness to the world of how God created us to relate to him, each other and the world.

JOHN 17:20-23

[20]I ask not only on behalf of these, but also on behalf of those who will believe in me
through their word, [21]that they may all be one. As you, Father, are in me and I am in
you, may they also be in us, so that the world may believe that you have sent me.
[22]The glory that you have given me I have given them, so that they may be one, as
we are one, [23]I in them and you in me, that they may become completely one, so that
the world may know that you have sent me and have loved them even as you have
loved me.

Questions

1. What is the relationship of the church to God, to each other and to the community?

2. What is the purpose of the church?

3. What does it mean to be a missional church?

Missional Community: Primary Characteristics* 13

Welcoming Environment

In a culture where everyone wants a place to belong, we have to have a welcoming environment for the newcomer. Within this environment the newcomer can see and experience the gospel.

Unity of Larger Church Community

Though the world is fractured into "tribal" groups, we in the church are called by God to be unified. It is a necessity, not an option.

Intimacy in Smaller Communities

While we are called to greater unity, we have a deep need for a more intimate community. We need to make sure we have established smaller groups of people who know each other on a deeper level.

Transformed Lives

Within these intimate communities in the church, individuals are transformed. God created us in his image to relate to him and each other in community.

Building Multiethnic Partnerships

In today's society, which is full of exclusive cultural communities, the church must work to make sure it has partnerships (and when possible communities) that are multiethnic so we can experience the fullness of God's creation, which is a multiethnic creation.

Proclaiming the Gospel by Word and Deed in Local and International Communities

In an emerging culture that struggles with accepting the truth, it's critical to proclaim the gospel by word and deed so people not only hear the gospel but see it also.

Missional Community: Questions to Consider

- How welcoming is our church or ministry to newcomers, including people from other ethnicities?

- What hampers us from being a more unified church?

- How effective are our ministry structures in developing transformed lives in intimate communities?

- What ways can we better live out the gospel in word and deed in our surrounding community? In the world?*

F. EXPERIENCING GOD (10-20 MINUTES)

For many years it was thought that Generation X and other generations that have been influenced by emerging, postmodern phenomena were not open to the gospel. But we have found that these emerging generations are very spiritual. Even Doug Coupland, who coined the phrase Generation X, has a hunger to experience God.

STEVE HAYNER INTERVIEW 15

EXPERIENCING GOD: BIBLICAL TEXT

BACKGROUND

This psalm was written in the context of David and Israel's struggle in a time of great tumult surrounding the nation of Israel. Great changes were ahead of them.

PSALM 46:1-7 16-17

1 God is our refuge and strength,
  a very present help in trouble.
2 Therefore we will not fear, though the earth should change,
  though the mountains shake in the heart of the sea;
3 though its waters roar and foam,
  though the mountains tremble with its tumult. *Sēl'ah*

4 There is a river whose streams make glad the city of God,
  the holy habitation of the Most High.
5 God is in the midst of the city; it shall not be moved;
  God will help it when the morning dawns.
6 The nations are in an uproar, the kingdoms totter;
  he utters his voice, the earth melts.
7 The LORD of hosts is with us;
  the God of Jacob is our refuge.

BIBLE STUDY QUESTIONS 18

1. What would a newcomer say your church takes refuge in?

2. Why does the psalmist say we should not fear?

3. In this psalm, how does God help his people?

4. How have you (your church or ministry) experienced God's presence in the past?

5. What needs to change so you and your church or ministry can experience God's presence now and in the future?

EXPERIENCING GOD: PRIMARY CHARACTERISTICS* 19

Community Context

The modern world and the modern church are centered around the individual. As we have come to understand the communal nature of the triune God, we understand that community is the primary context in which we should experience God.

Taking Time

To experience God takes time. We need to make sure in this hectic world that we don't get caught up with the phrenetic pace of life and not take the time to experience God.

Experiencing, Not Just Knowing About, God

In the modern world, we spent much of our time gaining knowledge about God. While that is a worthy goal, we need to make sure we emphasize experience with God, not just knowledge about God.

Practicing the Presence of God

Ever since Reformation times, many Protestant Christians have shied away from certain liturgies or Christian practices, such as *lectio divina* and the *Benedictine Rules*. We need to recover some of these practices that can lead us to a deepening experience of God.

Refuge in the Midst of Turmoil

Some of the best times to experience God and deepen our relationship with him are during times of greatest turmoil, as Psalm 46 describes.

Call to Dependence on the Holy Spirit

As we move out of a modern culture that taught us to be self-reliant, we need to make sure that we don't hold on to our stubborn self-reliance and fear of trusting others. We need to experience God by being willing to let the Holy Spirit guide and direct us.

Remembering the Past, Expecting the Future

Too often all we can see is our present situation. But Christians need to see the world from God's perspective. We need to understand his work in the past and have a certain hope and humble faith about his actions in the future. As one Christian leader said, "We need to see the present from a future perspective because we have seen God's faithfulness in the past."

EXPERIENCING GOD: QUESTIONS TO CONSIDER 20

- In our church or ministry, where do we as a community experience God? Where do I individually experience God?
- How does our church or ministry create an environment where people can experience God?*
- Would our church or ministry be better known for experiencing God or for dispensing knowledge about God?
- In what ways can I help our congregation or ministry members experience God in a deeper way?

G. RECONCILING GOSPEL (10-20 MINUTES)

ALEX GEE INTERVIEW 21

RECONCILING GOSPEL: BIBLICAL TEXT

BACKGROUND

The apostle Paul is speaking to the church in Corinth that has splintered into many quarrelsome groups. In this passage he is trying to challenge the Christian Corinthians to be reconciled to God and to each of the other ethnic groups that were represented in the Corinthian church.

2 Corinthians 5:14-18

[14]For the love of Christ urges us on, because we are convinced that one has died for all; 22-23
therefore all have died. [15]And he died for all, so to that those who live might live no
longer for themselves, but for him who died and was raised for them.
[16]From now on, therefore, we regard no one from a human point of view; even though
we once knew Christ from a human point of view, we know him no longer in that way.
[17]So if anyone is in Christ, there is a new creation: everything old has passed away; see,
everything has become new! [18]All of this is from God, who reconciled us to himself
through Christ, and has given us the ministry of reconciliation.

Bible Study Questions 24

1. According to the passage, why did Jesus die?

2. As a result of our reconciliation with God, how are we to view others?

3. Why did God give us the ministry of reconciliation?

4. Why might a multiethnic ministry be a crucial part of the ministry of reconciliation today?

5. What would a multiethnic ministry of reconciliation look like in our church or ministry?

Reconciling Gospel: Primary Characteristics* 25

Freedom from Shame and Guilt

We first need to be reconciled with God. For many people from the modern culture, the stumbling block in reconciliation with God is a sense of guilt: I have done something wrong. For many in the emerging culture the greatest struggle is with shame: There's something wrong with me. God through his reconciling gospel can give us freedom from both guilt and shame.

Freedom to Forgive Ourselves and Others

To be reconciled, those of us from a shame-based culture need to forgive ourselves because of Christ's forgiveness. Those of us from a guilt-based culture need to forgive others.

Called to Understand and Value Other Cultural and Ethnic Communities

The gospel's reconciling purpose is not fulfilled if I am only reconciled to God and people like myself. God, who created our ethnicities, desires us to be reconciled across ethnic and cultural lines.

Called to Fight for Justice

Part of that reconciliation across ethnic lines also includes standing up for what is right, and fighting against injustices against other ethnicities and people groups.

RECONCILING GOSPEL: QUESTIONS TO CONSIDER

- Why are we moving from a guilt-based culture to a shame-based culture?

- What implications does this change have for how we minister in the church? Outside the church?

- What opportunities does our church or ministry have to be part of a multiethnic ministry?*

- What prevents our church or ministry from moving forward in this area?

H. GREAT COMMANDMENT WITNESS (10-20 MINUTES)

TONY WARNER INTERVIEW

GREAT COMMANDMENT WITNESS: BIBLICAL TEXT

BACKGROUND

The religious leaders' goal is to trick Jesus. But his answer wasn't one they were expecting.

MATTHEW 22:36-40

36"Teacher, which commandment in the law is the greatest?" 37[Jesus] said to him, "'You
shall love the Lord your God with all your heart, and with all your soul, and with all your
mind.' 38This is the greatest and first commandment. 39And a second is like it: 'You shall
love your neighbor as yourself.' 40On these two commandments hang all the law and the
prophets."

Bible Study Questions

1. Why does Jesus say this commandment is the greatest?
2. What prevents me, my church or my ministry from loving God? From loving our neighborhood?

Great Commandment Witness: Primary Characteristics* 29

Perform Acts of Kindness

If people today are going to listen to the gospel message, they need to see Christians living out God's love in their actions. They want to see Christians not just "talking the talk" but "walking the walk." They need to see us making a difference in the surrounding community.

Demonstrate God's Love, Not Just Humankind's Tolerance

Tolerance merely calls us to be willing to put up with each other. This is actually of low value. God doesn't call us to tolerate our neighbor but to love our neighbor.

Provide a Place for Seekers to Belong

In the emerging culture most seekers are looking for a place to belong first. Then they look for a belief system compatible with their community. We need to make sure our church community is a place where seekers are welcomed.

Assist Seekers in Discovering How Their Story Fits into God's Kingdom Story

We need to help people see that no matter what their life story entails, not only does God understand, but their story fits into the larger story of God's creation, redemption and the final consummation of the world.

Challenge Seekers to Be Converted to Christ and Not Just to the Christian Community

In the emerging culture we need to make sure that seekers are not just converted to the Christian community. They need to recognize that Christ is the King of that community; thus we all have to commit to him as King of every member of the community.

Great Commandment Witness: Questions to Consider 30

- Why is the Great Commandment a more effective strategy than the Great Commission in the emerging culture?
- What role does Christian community have in a witness strategy to the emerging culture?
- What would a witness strategy look like if based on the Great Commandment?

- How does our church or ministry need to change its witness strategy to remain faithful to the gospel and yet be effective in the emerging culture?*

I. IMAGINATIVE WORSHIP (10-20 MINUTES)

SALLY MORGENTHALER INTERVIEW 

IMAGINATIVE WORSHIP: BIBLICAL TEXT

BACKGROUND
The author of Romans is laying the groundwork for how the Roman Christians (and us) should live their lives in the midst of hardships. The Christian's focus is centered on God, not on life's circumstances.

ROMANS 11:34—12:1 32

34 “For who has known the mind of the Lord?
Or who has been his counselor?”
35 “Or who has given a gift to him,
to receive a gift in return?
36 For from him and through him and to him are all things. To him be the
glory forever. Amen.
1 I appeal to you therefore, brothers and sisters, by the mercies of God, to present your
bodies as a living sacrifice, holy and acceptable to God which is our spiritual worship.

BIBLE STUDY QUESTIONS

1. Why do we focus on God in worship?

2. How is the presentation of our bodies a form of worship?

3. How is our view of worship too limited today?

IMAGINATIVE WORSHIP: PRIMARY CHARACTERISTICS* 

God-focused
In a culture that is still focused on the self, we need to make sure our focus is centered on God. We are called to worship God with our whole being.

Sacramental Foundation
In a culture that is image based and that desires to be connected to the past, baptism and communion are critical elements of worship.

Community-based

Worship should not be based primarily on our own individual identity but our community identity as a church.

Authentic

While excellence in our worship may be helpful, authenticity is much more important to God and to the seekers in our midst. We need to be real people who share all our emotions.

Participation by All

In worship our purpose is not centered on performance by a few but participation by all. We all are to present our bodies as living sacrifices.

Use of All Senses and Traditions

We need to be open to the use of all our senses in worship and open to other traditions with which we might not feel comfortable.

Changing Hearts

Worship should change our heart as well as our mind. Our different traditions tend to emphasize one over the other. God calls us to emphasize both heart and mind.

Witness to the Surrounding Communities

Worship can be a very powerful witness to postmoderns who desire to belong, are open to spirituality and long to experience God. As we consider the forms of our worship, we should not primarily consider our own interests but those forms of worship that connect with the surrounding communities.

Imaginative Worship: Questions to Consider

- Why do we so often center worship discussions around our personal desires and not the purposes of the church?

- How would our worship look different if we centered it on glorifying God and being a witness to the surrounding community? How are these two goals compatible?*

- How does our attitude toward worship need to change?

- What structures do we need to change?

J. NARRATIVE PREACHING (10-20 MINUTES)

BRIAN MCLAREN INTERVIEW

NARRATIVE PREACHING: BIBLICAL TEXT

BACKGROUND

This Scripture gives us a picture (story) of what our future life will be like. People today need these images to give them hope in the midst of today's world.

REVELATION 21:1-5

Then I saw a new heaven and a new earth; for the first heaven and the first earth had
passed away, and the sea was no more. [2]And I saw the holy city, the new Jerusalem, coming down out of heaven from God, prepared as a bride adorned for her husband. [3]And I
heard a loud voice from the throne saying,

"See, the home of God is among mortals.
He will dwell with them as their God;
they will be his peoples,
and God himself will be with them;
[4]he will wipe every tear from their eyes.
Death will be no more;
mourning and crying and pain will be no more,
for the first things have passed away."

[5]And the one who was seated on the throne said, "See, I am making all things new." Also, he said, "Write this, for these words are trustworthy and true."

BIBLE STUDY QUESTIONS

1. Why are story and image so critical in preaching in the emerging culture?

2. How would you have described the image that is presented in this passage?

3. What are the doctrines represented behind the image?

4. What would have been lost if this passage was given in a theoretical manner?

NARRATIVE PREACHING: PRIMARY CHARACTERISTICS*

Embedded in a Larger Worship Experience

Instead of being the primary focus in our worship services today, preaching, though very important, should be one part of the larger worship experience.

Multiple Preaching Voices
Because God's Word, and not the preacher, is authoritative and because many people have received the gift of preaching or teaching, we need multiple preaching voices in our congregation.

Development of Trust with the Audience
Since positional authority is progressively less important in the emerging culture, the preacher or teacher needs to develop trust with the audience over time to be effective. Preachers and teachers need to share stories from their own life journey so the congregation can identify with the messenger *and* the message.

Conversational Style
Postmodern people identify with and respond to the message of a speaker when he or she uses a more conversational than oratory communication style.

Use of Word and Image
As we move to an image-based culture, we need to recognize God has communicated in images since the beginning of time. Communicators of God's Word need to make use of images to not only meet people where they are but to fully and accurately communicate God's story.

Connect the Audience's Story with God's Kingdom Story
People today need to see that God is relevant to their own life situation *and* that their life is part of a much bigger picture. They need to envision how their life fits in God's kingdom story.

Mission-focused
A large part of God's kingdom story is God's mission. In our preaching and teaching we must not narrowly focus on our individual life or our local-church situation. We need to focus on God's mission and God's role for us in accomplishing his mission.

NARRATIVE PREACHING: QUESTIONS TO CONSIDER

- Why is it especially important to gain the audience's trust today?
- Why should we focus on both word and image in preaching?*
- Why is it helpful to have a variety of people preaching or teaching over time?
- What are the strengths of preaching or teaching in our church or ministry?
- What changes need to be made?

K. GOD'S KINGDOM STORY (10-20 MINUTES)

DIETER ZANDER INTERVIEW

GOD'S KINGDOM STORY: BIBLICAL TEXT

BACKGROUND

When Jesus rose to speak, no one in attendance had any idea he would make the statements he made. Jesus was beginning a mission that was much larger than anyone imagined. His mission was not focused on Israel or the world but on God's kingdom.

LUKE 4:16-21

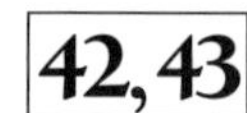

[16]When he came to Nazareth, where he had been brought up, he went to the synagogue
on the sabbath day, as was his custom. He stood up to read, [17]and the scroll of the prophet
Isaiah was given to him. He unrolled the scroll and found the place where it was written:
[18]"The Spirit of the Lord is upon me,
because he has anointed me
to bring good news to the poor.
He has sent me to proclaim release to the captives
and recovery of sight to the blind,
to let the oppressed go free,
[19]to proclaim the year of the Lord's favor."
[20]And he rolled up the scroll, gave it back to the attendant, and sat down. The eyes of
all in the synagogue were fixed on him. [21]Then he began to say to them, "Today this scripture has been fulfilled in your hearing."

BIBLE STUDY QUESTIONS

1. In what ways has God released you from captivity?

2. From this passage, what have you learned about God's kingdom story?

3. How has your church or ministry lived out this story among its members? Within the community?

4. Imagine that your church or ministry fulfilled this passage today. What would it look like?

GOD'S KINGDOM STORY: PRIMARY CHARACTERISTICS*

45

Turn from Focusing on Ourselves or Our Ministry to Focusing on God and His Purposes

Too often we focus only on or own needs. We need to stop looking at ourselves or our church members or ministry partners and look to God for our direction.

Recognize That We Are Part of a Larger Purpose

We don't look to God primarily for how he can help us but for what role he has for us in the development of his kingdom.

Continue to Understand God's Kingdom Story for Ourselves and Others

Our understanding of and our role in furthering God's kingdom is a lifelong journey. We must not become complacent or self-satisfied.

Commit to Helping Further God's Kingdom in Our Church and Our Communities

God has a role for all of us individually and communally in advancing his kingdom. He has graciously given us different gifts toward that end.

Confident Hope That God's Kingdom Will Be Fully Established in the Future

We can have full confidence that God's kingdom will be fully established in the future. This confident hope should comfort us in the present as we continue to expect God to accomplish his purposes—even when we can't see evidence of that work at a particular time.

God's Kingdom Story: Questions to Consider 46

- How should we characterize God's kingdom?

- How has our church or ministry already appropriated God's kingdom in daily life?

- In what ways does our church or ministry demonstrate God's kingdom? In what ways doesn't it?*

- What role does God have for our church or ministry in advancing his kingdom?

- What causes us to have hope in the future establishment of God's kingdom?

L. EMERGING HOPE (5-10 MINUTES)

As we conclude this curriculum, I hope that we will not only have a better understanding of the emerging culture and how it affects our ministry, but also that we have a strengthened hope that God is at work and has a role for all of us and our ministries to play in accomplishing his purposes.

JIMMY LONG INTERVIEW*

"God is calling us to be a people of hope who offer this gospel of hope to a culture without hope. We begin by caring for people in the emerging culture as real people with real hurts. We need to meet each other where we are and listen to each other's stories. Next, we must be praying that God will give us wisdom to know how to demonstrate God's love by word and deed and that God will draw this culture to himself. Finally, we must be sharing ourselves and the hope of the gospel within this culture so that people will begin to understand that God loves them and desires to give them a home they have never had, a place to belong. We also need to understand that it is only God who can provide this hope for discovering life's meaning, purpose and direction." (Jimmy Long, *Emerging Hope: A Strategy for Reaching the Postmodern Generations*) 47

Let's conclude our time by praying together as a community. Let's pray for the following:

- Thank God that he is actively involved in accomplishing his purposes.
- For a continued understanding of this emerging culture.
- For openness to changing ministry structures and strategies as God directs.
- For direction and wisdom in how to help our church or ministry to make the necessary changes.
- For our strengthened hope in a trustworthy and sovereign God and our continued faithfulness to him.

FURTHER RESOURCES 48

Website address: www.emergingculture.com
E-mail: emerginghope@aol.com

Acknowledgments

I would like to thank four sets of people in the completion of this *Emerging Culture Curriculum Kit*. First, I would like to thank Steve Hayner, former president, and Alec Hill, present president, of InterVarsity Christian Fellowship/USA for encouraging me as the coordinator of a team of InterVarsity staff in the development of the curriculum. The team members included Brian Housman (point person for the communications module), Rachelle McClintock (point person for the leadership module), Rick Richardson (point person for the witness module), Tony Warner (point person for the context module), Scott Anderson, Bora Reed, Rick Mattson and Brian Parks.

I also want to thank all the participants in the theological and practitioner consultations we held as we developed this material. I am indebted to the various seminary classes, church and parachurch leaders who participated in a variety of seminars I led using parts of the curriculum over the last few years. Your input and encouragement were invaluable.

It was a delight partnering with InterVarsity Press and Twentyonehundred Productions in the assembling of this curriculum. Drew Blankman and Cindy Bunch of InterVarsity Press contributed endless hours of editing of the material. Pete Luisi-Mills and Scott Wilson and numerous other members of 2100 shared their creative and technological expertise in the development of all the PowerPoint and videos for the curriculum.

I also want to thank the Maclellan Foundation (along with three other foundations) and my home church, the Chapel Hill Bible Church, for being financially committed to this project. Without their generous gifts this project would not have been possible.